N E X T

VISIONS TOWARD A LESS-DIVIDED AMERICA

Edited by Artress Bethany White

Pangyrus

Cambridge, Massachusetts

Dedicated to Grace Segran, a gifted writer and treasured friend, who is dearly missed.

Next: Visions Toward a Less-Divided America, Pangyrus © 2022
All Stories © 2022
Attributed to the authors named herein, except when noted otherwise
ISBN: 978-0-9979164-9-2

For information about permission to reproduce selections from this book, please write to Permissions at info@pangyrus.com

Composition by Esther Weeks
Cover art by Louisa Bertman
Cover design by Douglas Woodhouse

Pangyrus
2592 Massachusetts Ave #2
Cambridge, MA 02140
pangyrus.com

CONTENTS

Letter from the Editor 5

About the Contest Winner 10

Playground Primer
Grace Segran 11

There's Nothing New About Normal
Anri Wheeler 27

Remembering the Forgotten: The Space that Remains
Amy Shea 37

She Wants to Lead
Ananda Lowe 73

A Murmuration of Stones
Robbie Gamble 94

On Being (Asian)
Justin Chen 103

Reading the Good News
Greg Harris 129

**Race, Family, and Enduring Histories: An Interview with
E. Dolores Johnson about her Memoir _Say I'm Dead_**
Artress Bethany White 145

**May You Rise To It: A Love Letter to Students
in an Unprecedented Time**
Timothy Patrick McCarthy 154

**Play Like a Girl
A Review of _Hail Mary: The Rise and Fall of the National Women's
Football League_**
Aime Card 171

Contributors 176

LETTER FROM THE EDITOR

_____

As I sit down to write this letter, recent weeks have brought many in this nation to collective dismay and rage against institutional powers restricting reproductive rights and the ability of communities to protect themselves legislatively against rampant gun violence. The seizuret of these critical rights is not accidental and reflects actions against the gains made toward social equity and bodily protections over the course of decades. Still, the search for truth and justice continues — such as the current hearings in regard to the January 6, 2021 attack on the nation's Capitol — and reveals that giving in to disinformation and other rhetorics of oppression is not an option. The way forward continues to be through brave stories that expose the divisions and injustices that we work to resist.

Stories are what are next, stories that reveal: the pain of gender and racial bias; the lack of empathy for economically marginalized and persons with disabilities; the confusion and grief in this era of pandemic and climate change. The essays gathered in this volume creatively interrogate history and traditionalist thinking to narratively chart a clear path toward change. Presented here are questions that demand a response and ask all of us to work toward a better tomorrow.

Several of the essays compiled here were finalists for our inaugural nonfiction contest and, fittingly, the first selection is contest-winner Grace Segran's "Playground Primer." Segran's prose explores the perilous nature of racial and ethnic bias among Europeans, Americans, and Asians living abroad and at home in the U.S. She unabashedly chronicles the realities of transracial families and their sometimes rocky origins: "My Chinese family cut me off when I married Raja, who was Indian, in 1979. In 2012, our daughter married a white American man from Atlanta whom we loved, at a wedding party that resembled the United Nations assembly." Segran's work is timely and resonant and contest judge Jabari Asim shares his statement on why he chose "Playground Primer" as the winner in this volume.

"Remembering the Forgotten: The Space That Remains" by Amy Shea and "A Murmuration of Stones" by Robbie Gamble both interrogate the history of cemeteries and society's willingness to discard the dead, specifically those from indigent and institutionalized populations. Within Shea's meticulously documented essay, readers discover that indeed "dignity isn't free" when it comes to burial; in fact some with no wealth or status in our society are fated to be interred within a potter's field. Shea goes on to indict America for its mistreatment of the homeless while also revealing that homelessness moves far too easily from the natural world to the grave in unexpected ways. Gamble also divulges the anonymity that prevailed unto death for the socially silenced in his nuanced, lyric essay. He traces the history of the Fernald School founded in 1848 for "cognitively-challenged children on a campus of grim, red-brick institutional buildings" which was once the site of horrific eugenic practices.

After more than two years in the on-again off-again throes of COVID-19, it is refreshing to look at how we have weathered the onslaught at school and at home in essays by Timothy Patrick McCarthy and Anri Wheeler. McCarthy's "Letter to My Students" is a poignant look at how the pandemic placed educators in the position of mental health advocates for despondent students. It is heartfelt and heartbreaking in the way it uncovers the extent to which educators can choose to participate in the future aspirations of young adults, including imbuing them with the will to survive.

Wheeler's "There's Nothing New About Normal" takes a different perspective on the pandemic by considering the extreme views around child vaccination practices. Turning away from selfish individualism, she asks for a more community-based approach:

> "This is the world I want for my daughters. As more species go extinct, and more ice melts into the rising seas, I want them to reach for each other. To know people who wish to build with them, to connect across geographies and decades with no ulterior motive beyond asking questions and actually wanting to hear honest answers."

I fell in love with Ananda Lowe's essay "She Wants to Lead" for its cultural richness and determination to upend traditional gender roles. The author's passion in describing what it means to be female and have the desire to lead in a traditionally male-led dance form mixes with her passion for the dance itself: "When it is *bachata* night at the club, there is a difference in the air from salsa nights. Each song begins with the deep, rolling sound of an electric guitar, as if the instrument is licking its own lips in anticipation of what will come next." The sensuality of Lowe's prose does not stop there and is truly a rhythmic, immersive experience.

Finally, in "On Being (Asian)" by Justin Chen, the writer takes a probing look at his identity in the face of anti-Asian hate crimes at the national level: "Growing up, I've been aware of my Asianness but, until this year, I've never thought deeply about my race or ethnicity. Within my middle-class life in a liberal city, I've floated through a frictionless and illusory world of equals." His world is shattered when he must reassess his communal consciousness by resurrecting memories of what he once thought it meant to be part of an immigrant family from Taiwan.

Bonus reads in this nonfiction collection include a response to climate change initiatives penned by *Pangyrus* founding editor Greg Harris; a review of *Hail Mary: The Rise and Fall of the National Women's Football League* (2021) by Associate Nonfiction Editor Aime Card; and an interview with E. Dolores Johnson about the writing of her memoir *Say I'm Dead: A Family Memoir of Race, Secrets, and Love* (2020) by yours truly.

I would be remiss if I did not applaud the fabulous cover image by visual artist Louisa Bertman. *Next* is about collective efforts, and Bertman adroitly captures the personality and beauty of all of the writers who made this special issue possible.

While it is difficult to be hopeful for America at this divisive time, these visions of a more sympathetic, empathic, connected country do lift my spirits. I hope they lift yours as well. Enjoy!

Artress Bethany White

Pangyrus Nonfiction Editor

About The Contest Winner

Jabari Asim, Judge of Pangyrus Nonfiction Contest 2021

In "Playground Primer," Grace Segran interrogates her experiences with otherness as an adopted mixed-race child in Malaysia and as an adult racial minority in the Philippines, various European countries and, most tellingly, in the United States. She navigates schoolrooms, workplaces, and playgrounds, each of which reveals additional complexities of racial discrimination. With her home life as a wife and mother providing a valuable refuge, she pits her persistent optimism and self-reliance against harmful assumptions and stubborn ignorance. In patient, eloquent prose, she offers a heedful warning that we must challenge prejudice directly, that globalization and the high-speed spread of information are not enough to overcome long-standing divisions by themselves.

Playground Primer
Grace Segran

A month after we relocated to Paris in the summer of 1989, our daughter, Elizabeth, started first grade at the International School of Paris. *Et alors*, after school the first day, the mothers brought their kids down to *jardin du Ranelagh*. Elizabeth and I went along, hoping to get to know other parents and their children. I watched her playing from the shade of the oak tree. She stood out prominently with her father's South Indian dark skin tone, as she played with white European and American kids on the swings and slide.

An American mother in a crisp linen shirt dress with a sun hat and a monogrammed L.L. Bean canvas tote bag walked over to me.

"Hi. Are you Elizabeth's nanny?" she asked.

I smiled. "I'm afraid not. I'm her mom."

She gushed apologies.

"Do you live close by?" she asked awkwardly, trying to make conversation.

"A twenty-minute walk from school, in Passy. What about you?"

"We live just down the street from school."

Shortly after, the mom moved away to join a fellow American who had just arrived with her son. I noticed a younger woman following close behind her who looked a lot like me — brown skin, black hair, no makeup, sandals, shapeless knee-length skirt, untucked peasant top. I found out the following day that the young woman was the school mom's domestic helper whom she had brought from their previous posting in Manila.

When Raja, my husband, got home that evening, he wanted to know how Elizabeth's first day went. I mentioned in passing my encounter with the American mom at the playground.

"How did that make you feel?" he asked. I knew he was concerned because it was synonymous with being asked if I were the maid. In Malaysia, where we were born and bred, the hired help lived in and did household chores as well as took care of the children of middle- and upper-class families (socio-economic brackets that Raja's family and mine didn't qualify for). My family at least had food on the table. Raja was lucky if he got one decent meal a day when he was growing up.

"I wasn't expecting such a question," I said, "but I wasn't upset nor felt humiliated. In fact, I was slightly amused."

I wondered why I was nonchalant about being called a maid. Didn't bat an eyelid. Why was I not offended by the question?

This is probably why. Raja and I were the minority racial groups in Malaysia and were discriminated against by the Malaysian Constitution that required the government set quotas for the dispensation of scholarships, employment in the civil service and the private sector, housing, and land ownership. The law favored the Malays with the intention of improving their economic status and participation.

When the 1971 New Economic Policy was implemented, we were in middle school, soon to enter high school, college, and the workforce. We were not able to get scholarships to go to university. Raja managed to scrape together financial contributions from his eldest brother and a cousin, received a small bursary provided by the Indian Association, and was admitted as a super-freshman straight into second year, thereby saving a year of tuition fees and living expenses. He was unable, however, to get a job after grad school and looked further afield in neighboring Singapore, which operated on a meritocracy policy. There, socio-economic mobility was made possible through hard work and ability, regardless of ethnicity. He got a job with Singapore Airlines and rose quickly in the company.

I endured a different type of discrimination as an adopted child in a home with a couple who already had three older children of their own. I was adopted by my natural mother's brother when she died giving birth to me. My adoptive parents favored their own children. And they showed it. That emboldened my siblings. I was marginalized and became the other: the one they didn't really want. There was often no mercy or justice when there was conflict between my siblings and me. Grace — unmerited favor — was difficult to come by, if at all. I learned from a very young age not to expect anything from anybody. If I wanted something, I had to earn it. Make it happen myself.

That philosophy prepared me for when I had to deal with issues in the real world. I was not eligible for a college scholarship despite good grades because I was of Chinese heritage. My Malay friends were showered with handsome stipends and full scholarships and sent overseas, albeit often with help from the government to get a place in the university. At work, I reported to a manager, who barely got through high school. She was offered the higher position by virtue of her ethnicity — sanctioned by the national employment policy.

So I settled. I accepted the situation I didn't want and that which I couldn't have. Made peace with my lot in life and used whatever agency I had to improve my life. I didn't become a lawyer or study literature as I had dreamed but worked my way up to become a registered nurse. I would never become the director of the nursing division — such high-level positions were reserved for Malays, but I had a job. I was in a good place, all things considered.

I had good childhood friends who were Malay and whom I loved. I didn't envy them. It was their good fortune to be born on the right side of the economic policy. The fact that they benefited from the policy and I didn't never came between us in our relationship. It just was. Life continued genially on a level social playing field and an unequal economic one.

Raja's job took us all over the world. We were always in the minority group, but I was not intimidated by that, integrating with gay abandon with the locals. I often forgot that I bore a different skin color and culture, and spoke with a weird accent. Racial discrimination was not the first thing that came to mind when someone said things that could be interpreted as racist, which was why the playground question didn't faze me. It didn't bother me to be called a nanny so much as it piqued my interest in the reasons for the assumption, the way I investigated my subjects when covering a human-interest story for my editor.

It was an unusual thing to ask someone if she's the nanny, I thought, though I couldn't say precisely why it felt unusual. I pondered that remark for several days afterwards. What does a nanny look like? I wasn't in a nanny uniform as some employers expect of their help. Was it the casual way I dressed? But the way I dressed didn't define my identity. I chose comfort and ease of grooming over sophistication anytime, except when I was at a social event or official function that required a formal dress code. Was it because Elizabeth and I looked racially different? We had different skin tones and facial features: hers were South Indian like Raja's and mine were more Filipino-esque, coming from Maritime Southeast Asia (also known in the 16th Century as *The East Indies* and in the 18th Century as the *Malay Archipelago* in history books) which included Malaysia and the Philippines. And because many Filipinas had gone abroad as immigrant domestic helpers, was the assumption that I must be the nanny to a foreigner? If Elizabeth and I had the same skin tone and features, would the school mom still have thought so?

Back home in Malaysia, no one assumed I was the maid just because our family unit was composed of different races. Neither did I encounter it when we lived in Manila or Jakarta where I could blend into a crowd. Two years before Paris, like the school mom, we had also been posted to Manila. Although a Malaysian of Chinese descent with 25 percent Thai blood, I was frequently mistaken to be Filipina. That flattered me. It meant I was considered one of them. I belonged. I felt safe riding in jeepneys and shopping in the wet markets in Manila.

Being brown and vastly different-looking than Raja and Elizabeth didn't prompt the nanny question either when we lived among white people in Belgium, the U.K., and France, except for the school mom at the Parisian playground. But then she was American.

Our downstairs neighbor in Paris, Fanny Ardant, was delightful, chatting with us in the hallway and asking us how we were settling in or telling us in the fall that the oyster man had set up shop at our street corner. She even mischievously took the liberty to play our piano when the deliverymen stopped to catch their breath in front of her *appartement*. We later found that she was the femme fatale of French cinema whose partner was François Truffaut, the renowned film director. For whatever reason, her celebrity status didn't affect her treatment of us. She was simply the girl-next-door, gracious *et très génial* and didn't seem to notice we were brown or our lack of sophistication and *savoir-vivre*.

Was it a white American phenomenon to assume one is a nanny because of one's looks or skin color?

I recall our visit to Beaufort, SC four years earlier in 1985. We attended adult Bible class before church service. The folks in the class and the service afterwards were pure white, except for the three of us who stood out like sore thumbs. The teacher, probably trying to make us feel welcomed by including us in the class activities, thought he would ask Raja to read the Bible passage aloud, however, he prefaced the request with "Can you read?" I saw Raja suppressing a smile, somewhat tickled by the question. "I'll try my best," he said. He then proceeded to read with gentle eloquence in the same manner he spoke his lines as John Proctor in *The Crucible* in high school or when he led business meetings at work.

We were rather bemused by the Sunday school teacher's question. We had been introduced to the class by the Capps, our hosts, who were missionaries in Malaysia and were home on furlough. Growing up in a British colony, we spoke English as our first language. We only spoke our mother tongue at home — Tamil for Raja and the Hokkien dialect for me — and rather poorly at that. Our mother tongues were peppered liberally with English words. We thought Americans were more informed about the world than us Southeast Asians. Our people were generally poorer so we were less educated — only a few of our cohort could afford to go to university; less read — English books were imported and expensive; and less traveled — most Southeast Asians at that time had never been on a plane. If Raja hadn't worked for an airline and received travel privileges, we likely wouldn't have traveled at all. It appeared that the folks at the Beaufort church were not so well-traveled either.

"They've probably never seen the likes of us," Raja said after the class when we were alone.

"Does it mean they think we live in trees?" I asked.

"Possibly. It's a stereotype of people from the Far East, I suppose. Primitive. Preliterate."

The ignorance was sobering.

However, the Paris school mom was highly educated, well-traveled, lived in our part of the world, and married to a high-ranking European man who worked in the Asian Development Bank (the equivalent of the World Bank in Asia). Thus, the nanny question was bewildering. I didn't expect someone with her global experience to ask such a question.

One theory I had for the phenomenon was that perhaps the Belgians, French, and English were at ease with foreigners like us because they were cognizant of other races through their colonies in the recent past. I am not saying colonization is good, only that it afforded knowledge of, and even experience with, another race.

The Belgian Empire included the Congo from 1902 till 1960. Belgium was our first posting outside of Asia. We had two tours of duty there. In our first tour in 1987, my Belgian French teacher spoke fondly of life in Kinshasa and the bush where she was born and lived till she came back for college. We returned twenty years later for another tour and, while the younger generation of Belgians did not have direct experience with colonial life, they knew a lot about it through their parents and grandparents.

After Belgium, we moved to Paris and our white French friends spoke knowledgeably about cultures from French North and West Africa, the Caribbean, Indochina, and beyond. They also tended to go on vacation in those countries and the surrounding areas.

Most Brits knew Malaysia well. For example, on our first tour of duty in London in 2001, our B&B host in the Cotswolds, a pretty pocket of rural England, had actually been to our neck of the woods. On our second tour of duty in 2008, our landlady in Hammersmith told us she grew up in Sungai Petani in our state of Kedah, a small town 30 miles from where Raja and I lived till we completed Form Six (high school). Her dad was the head of the public utilities department during British rule. Coincidentally, her wifi password was 'Kedah.' Incredibly random experiences but it showed that the Brits were aware of, and even loved life, in our part of the world.

There are more interracial marriages today than during our time. My Chinese family cut me off when I married Raja, who was Indian, in 1979. In 2012, our daughter married a white American man from Atlanta, whom we loved. The wedding party resembled the United Nations assembly, friends along with their partners and spouses of all shades and colors and from different continents. The unconventional had become conventional. To cut the Paris mom some slack, the encounter with her took place in 1989. It is now 2020 and globalization has taken place. People are crisscrossing the globe regularly and reading widely on the internet. The playground scenario, one might imagine, must be history. Apparently not.

In March 2017, the BBC "Dad, Interrupted" video went viral when South Korea expert Robert Kelly was gatecrashed by his two little children during an interview. Thousands upon thousands of viewers assumed the Korean woman who swooped in to salvage the situation was his nanny or maid. I didn't. Not even for a second. I was more concerned for the poor man's reputation and applauded his wife for her valiant act.

I wondered if there were similar conversations out there about the roles played by non-white women in mixed race marriages here in America. I googled "Are you the nanny?" and many links came up that led to many more. There was creativity in the question these days and such incidents occur not only in the playground but everywhere. At the grocery store, school gate, and soccer practice.

Here are situations and variations of the question I found online.

- Poaching seems to be a regular motivator: "Are you working part-time for this family? We're looking for a new nanny and you're so loving with the child." Or "You take very good care of the child. Are you looking for a new job? I am looking for a new nanny."

- While her biracial child was playing in the sandbox, an Indian mom new to the area walked over to a white mom who was pushing her child on the swing. She smiled and said hello. Instead of receiving the friendly gesture in kind, the white mom said sternly, "Shouldn't you be doing your job and watch the kid instead of coming over to talk to me?"

- "Please tell his mom that this little cutie is so well-behaved," was said to a mom at the grocery check-out line.

- "Do they pay you extra to speak Vietnamese to the child?"
- "Did he just call you 'Mom'?!" takes the cake.
- "So nice of you to adopt a child!" Maybe not a nanny question, but predicates that you can't possibly be his mom because you look different.

It sometimes happens between moms of the same race. One Haitian mom with a biracial child was asked by another, "They treat you good?"

The assumption, though rare, has happened to a white mom with biracial children too. "Even though it's much more common for women of color to be asked the nanny question, it still stings," one mom wrote on a blog. "It's the offensive assumption our culture makes about class and race."

There are assumed role reversals when the nanny is white and the mom is brown. A Colombian scriptwriter and actress said that when she's out with her white nanny especially when she "hasn't put on make-up yet," people assume she's the nanny. This tends to happen more often in rich neighborhoods.

I wondered if dressing smartly — more smartly than women who are unmistakably the moms of the child they are with because they look like them — or speaking like an American would invite the assumption. Some moms wrote that it didn't matter how you dressed or how you spoke. "Once they see you are brown and have a lighter or darker child with you, you must be the nanny," said one mom who lived in an affluent neighborhood in Los Angeles.

These situations all occurred in the U.S., as far as I could tell. I wondered if it's the same in other countries? An Asian mom wrote, "I have never experienced people thinking I was the nanny until I moved here (U.S.) even though I've lived in Australia, France, and England. And suddenly there were nannies all around and they began to assume that I was one of them. They would sit with me and ask me if I was looking for another job or if I was working part-time."

It appears that these societal and socio-economic constructs are rampant, judging by media coverage and the moms who are blogging about it. Some people can't make sense of what they see before them and they slip into that construct. Some comments are even egregious and flagrant.

Enough already, I hear the moms saying. What is wrong with you? Have you not seen a multiracial family before? Is a multiracial family offensive to you? When they share the experience with a friend, they are told "You are being sensitive." "This is reality." People expect them to laugh it off. But some can't: "I gave birth to my baby and raised her and people don't recognize it." They are just tired of explaining to others why they don't look like their child. The fact is they shouldn't need to, but they have to because of white privilege and the biased thinking that families should all look the same. If the woman in the Robert Kelly video had blond hair and blue eyes, would viewers have assumed her to be the nanny? Not even for a second.

Three decades and seven cities around the world later, I still look the same. Brown skin, dark hair, no makeup. Casual, comfortable clothes. *Malheureusement*, five years in Paris, the fashion capital, didn't do any good for my presentation. The difference is I wear Allbirds now instead of Clarks, live in Cambridge, Massachusetts, and have a three-year-old granddaughter named Ella. Ella has her white father's porcelain skin and her mom's thick dark shoulder-length hair that bounces when she moves. Last week, I visited them at their home in Harvard Square. While her mom was running errands, Ella and I went to the neighborhood playground with my son-in-law. He read on the bench while I watched Ella play on the monkey bars. A white American mother sidled up to me and said: "Are you Ella's nanny?"

Paris suddenly didn't feel that long ago.

I thought I had graduated from the nanny question when

my daughter graduated from the playground. But my playground membership had been reactivated with the arrival of Ella. Then lightning struck again. In the same place. This time the stakes were lower — I'm one generation removed — but in another sense the stakes were higher because I've never been so racially conscious as I have since I moved to the U.S. I've learned, albeit very slowly, to respond to an invasive comment or line of questioning. I had a varicolored expostulation for the white woman but I didn't say it because it wouldn't be helpful. But I needed to let her know the question was inappropriate. So I shifted the responsibility of answering it back to her.

I smiled. "Why do you ask?"

"Hmm. Uh. I…uh…I thought…uh…," she floundered.

Lucky for her, Ella ran to me squealing "Grandma! Grandma!" and hugged my knee. I took her hand, her dad took the other, and we walked towards Harvard Square debating whether to stop at Burdick's for hot chocolate.

THERE'S NOTHING NEW ABOUT NORMAL

Anri Wheeler

I do not want a new normal. I crave an eradication of the concept of the norm. Normal is built upon exclusion and status quo. I ache for renewed curiosity — to live fully, in ways that don't require measurement against a template, obliterating the binaries that were constructed to allow for one group to more easily dominate another.

Ask me questions, give me space to grow, come eat mochi with me at my kitchen table.

*

It is late June. I am waiting for an elevator to take me and my towel-wrapped daughters back to our fifth-floor hotel room where our dog awaits our return. We have just been liberated from a 12-hour car ride and they have been enjoying the pool while I have been sipping the rooftop bar's Mezcal-based cocktail. Next to us stands a group of grey-haired white people, dressed in plain slacks and crisp polos and blouses. One of them asks why my children are masked.

"They're too young to be vaccinated..." my voice trails off. "There is a global…"

"Don't you DARE vaccinate them!" The woman who says this leans in. I see powder and pale blush, pooling in the creases of her unmasked face.

I knew this moment was coming. I didn't know the where or the how of it, but as we packed our car to the brim with clothes and snacks, downloading enough audiobooks to get us through the first days of the drive from Massachusetts to Washington state, I knew we would encounter some version of this woman. The only surprising part was that it took until Montana to happen.

"Have a good night." I waved the group towards the open elevator doors, signaling that we would wait for the next one, something I likely would have done anyway given the pandemic. The girls have a few more minutes to drip dry in the mountain air. My eldest, newly eleven, looks at me with concerned eyes. She is not accustomed to seeing me admonished in this way, later asking why the woman had such a strong reaction. The baby, who is five, leans her head against me as she grips my hand. She understands more than her body language reveals.

I have never considered myself patriotic. From the rote recitation of the Pledge of Allegiance at the start of every elementary school assembly, to the preponderance of flags waving on the Fourth of July, I've come to associate patriotism with rituals and holidays that have never felt inclusive of me; that were built on oppressive foundations. I know that some view social justice activism as its own form of patriotism. And while I agree when James Baldwin says, "I love America more than any other country in the world and, exactly for this reason, I insist on the right to criticize her perpetually," I can't shake my association of American patriotism with individualism. And what I yearn for, what I find most lacking in my life these days, is a collective. A genuine embodiment of Fannie Lou Hamer's "Nobody's free until everybody's free." I am a person who likes to build community, and so it's hard to feel rejected by, or not at home in, places where I've tried to do just that. Sometimes I feel this way about America itself.

*

My mother immigrated to the U.S. in her late twenties from Tokyo. She arrived with an open-ended return ticket and the singular goal of passing the competitive audition to become a Weeki Wachee mermaid. Which she did, becoming the first mermaid of color to swim in the cool, clear waters of the then thriving theme park. Years later, after returning home and meeting my white American father in a Tokyo bar, she married him and emigrated for good. Though she has lived in New York City longer than she has in Tokyo, she remains a green card holder with no desire to become a U.S. citizen. She uses the word "American" as a synonym for "white." This verbal inaccuracy is one of the many ways she has internalized what is considered the norm in the close to five decades she has spent here. My mother's voice runs through my head when I ponder what, if anything, unifies us, what we who claim the word American among our identifiers might share.

I would often correct Mama, explaining that people of all races can be American. Lately I've stopped. There is a truth to what she is saying, even if it's not what she means.

*

I used to view leaving New England as a panacea. That shaking off the chill I feel in this place I have lived for 15 years but will never refer to by the signifier "home," would somehow make everything okay. I still fantasize about constructing a cluster of tiny houses with my chosen family of friends and escaping there often. But more than that I crave feeling seen. Those moments when a text or a call from a friend fills my eyes because of how plainly they are reflecting parts of me back to myself, showing me who I am in a place that often succeeds at obscuring this vision. My people are scattered throughout the world; I remember when we were effortlessly concentrated and how I took for granted the ease with which we could gather.

Teenage clusters in my high school courtyard. Platonic snuggles on the twin XL beds of my college classmates. Summer camp nights under a tarp in the Pacific Northwest. Even the un-masked days of the not-so-distant past. Are they pure in my mind because of the filter of time, or because those were times when community lived up its meaning? Like anything, I know it is a combination of both. We clung to each other because we could, *and* we were all too willing to be vulnerable, to share new iterations of our still-forming selves.

Today I endure dinners and school functions where the conversations never penetrate deeper than pleasantries. A version of masks we all wore long before the cloth and surgical ones that help stave the spread of the latest variant. New England mores are a factor, yes, but so are age and socioeconomic class, and I have climbed in both. We tsk-tsk the cumulative injustices of the circles we inhabit, rarely naming our contributions. I used to bottle up then burst forth when enough rage or alcohol paved the way. I'm getting better at naming things in the moment, working to more regularly share the things that course through me. I write and teach about systems of oppression, sometimes for a wide audience, but find it hardest to disrupt them in my intimate circles. That is my complicity. I wish others could see theirs. I wish we could call each other out.

*

The day that five to twelve-year-olds (including my three daughters) are finally eligible to be vaccinated, there is so much activity across my mom group chats. Where did you book your shots?; Did you get a slot?; You need to plan shots to be safe for the holidays! Vaccination feels like yet another iteration of what I have come to know, and loathe, about many of my fellow parents. The need to be first, to get "the best" for one's kids at all costs, to post the perfect (post-jab) photo to Instagram. I am eager to get needles into my daughters' arms, which I know is the right thing to do, but I get swept up in the mad race, despite myself. I stay up late into the night refreshing my browser, trying to get them appointments, to no avail. I throw my phone across the couch, disappointed in myself, not because I didn't secure an appointment but because I know they will still get vaccinated long before so many in the U.S. and beyond. I am, again, wishing for something different that I can't quite articulate.

*

For close to two years my world has been flat. Because of the privilege of jobs that my partner and I were able to move remote, I have not set foot in a workplace or hosted anyone in my home since COVID made landfall in the U.S. Most of my friends and colleagues have been reduced to faces on a screen, rectangular boxes with backgrounds that have grown so familiar. I notice when people are not in their usual Zoom spots or have put up a new digital background. But we have been flattening each other long before early 2020. I rely on social media to keep me up to date on who has moved, partnered/unpartnered, or added children and pets to their lives, but I am increasingly alarmed at the battles that rage — stoked by a lack of actual dialogue — in the ever-spiraling comment sections and threads. I can't help but fall down rabbit holes of sub-threads and escalating exchanges. But I draw the line at participating. I save my energy for other tactics. When we reduce others to the words they type with two thumbs, often in heightened states, we are not seeing each other. We judge typos and autocorrects as if they are character flaws. We lack curiosity.

I am not defending internet trolls, or those who come online with the goal of tearing down others. I know the pain that results from virtual encounters where I wasn't my best self. Where I fucked up, and have worked hard to make amends. I have been implicated in rupturous conflicts that emerged in this 2-D world we are building as we go. Jobs lost, friendships ended, families fractured. Flattening has been an expediting force.

Whether or not we ever emerge more fully from a world bound by virtual rectangles, I hope that my daughters won't be reduced to others' interpretations of the photos they post on social media. That they are not dragged into comment section discourse that goes nowhere. I hope we can listen for nuance, and extend grace where accountability is genuine. There are models of this, and have been for centuries, they just haven't been the norm in a settler colonial America.

*

The day my girls get their first shots, I stay awake too late catching up on writing, and trashy TV, and life. When I finally get off the couch to go to bed, I check my phone one last time. A friend had posted a video to one of my camp friends' group chats. In it, a TikToker walks through someone's home speaking to the camera, "Real quick, if someone sent this to you, three things: One, they are proud of you. Two, they love you. And three, they are cheering for you. They are on your team." I smile. It is beyond cheesy. It is the kiss goodnight I didn't know I needed. It is the thing that makes me feel 3-dimensional, seen.

*

Andrew, a dear friend, likes to ask a second *how are you*, cutting past the automatic "okay" often tossed at the first. Another friend, Al, will call without pre-arranging a time. He will see me so vividly as we chat that I am often wiping away tears, unbeknownst to Al who continues our catch up. The entire call with Al is a second how are you. Ginny, who is a therapist and is old enough to be my mother, asks the most pointed, though unassuming, questions that immediately disarm me and I find myself sharing things I have told few others.

This is the world I want for my daughters. As more species go extinct, and more ice melts into the rising seas, I want them to reach for each other. To know people who wish to build with them, to connect across geographies and decades with no ulterior motive beyond asking questions and actually wanting to hear honest answers.

We are not the accomplishments of our offspring. We are not the institutions that have or haven't recognized us. We are the people with whom we laugh and cry and breathe and die. Mine live in Seattle, and Salt Lake City, and Boulder, and DC, and Providence. In Little Rock, and Baltimore, and Tokyo, and Johannesburg. In New York City, and Port Washington, and Cambridge. In LA and Oakland and San Francisco too. They are in my bones. Interactions with them remind me of who I have been and push me towards who I ache to be. They ask the questions that crack me open and place my shards on their palms, where they glisten.

REMEMBERING THE FORGOTTEN: THE SPACE THAT REMAINS

Amy Shea

Burying the Masses

On September 13th 2018, I stood in the county cemetery in my hometown of Fresno, California. It swam with more sheriff's employees than I could count. My dad and I parked on the street alongside Ararat Armenian Cemetery, then walked across the train tracks and street, passing a group of officers standing at the head of the dirt road into Fresno County Cemetery. We'd dressed up, my dad was in gray slacks and a button up short sleeve shirt and I was dressed head to toe in black. Even in a tank top, I realized that wearing black on a 95-degree, sunny day might have been a bad idea, but it felt necessary. We were here to show respect.

On this day the county was burying 740 cremains belonging to indigent people who'd died in Fresno County over the last nine years. Those labeled as indigent are defined as suffering from extreme poverty, lacking, deficient in something specified. Each set of cremains were stored in a 6-inch by 9-inch box, labeled, and placed within two coffin-sized wooden crates.

Prior to the 2018 service, the last mass burial at Fresno County Cemetery had been in 2009. The reasons for which were multiple. A few weeks prior to the ceremony date, the sheriff's department advertised the names of those to be buried, in the event that any family and friends wanted to claim their cremains before they were put in the ground, as once interred, cremains cannot be dug up. This notice went out far too late, and with such little time before the burial, the sheriff's department pushed all the names out onto their website and offered free reclamation of cremains if proof could be provided that you had a connection to the person you wished to take. Only sixty sets of cremains were ultimately paid for and claimed, leaving the county with 740 to be buried. The ad read:

Please call (559) 600 -3400 or email coroner@fresnosherrif.

org. The last day to collect was September 11, 2018.

Otherwise respects can be paid at 242 N. Hughes Avenue,

Fresno CA 93706: Plot #s 58 and 59 (Fresno Sheriff's Office).

Potter's Fields

The term 'potter's field' comes from the Bible (Matthew [27:7] in reference to a burial field bought by the Jews with the blood money, unsuitable for any other use, of Judas (Christian Apologetics and Research Ministry). The first time I saw the Fresno County Cemetery, which is Fresno's potter's field, was in the summer of 2010 when I accompanied my dad to the Holy Cross Cemetery on the corner of Belmont and Hughes, where my maternal great-grandparents were buried. In tracing and recording the genealogy of our family tree my dad wanted to take the pictures of their headstones so that he could upload them to the grave finding site, Findagrave.com: Facebook for the dead.

Upon retiring, my dad began working with the Fresno County Genealogical Society housed within the local library. He'd initially gotten involved with them as he worked on completing our family tree. He then became a volunteer, working on a project of mapping and cataloging cemeteries in Fresno and those individuals buried in them so that families and others could find them if they so wished.

This work eventually led him to the Fresno County Cemeteries and the coroner's office, which maintained the physical records he needed to complete his mapping and database of names for the cemeteries they owned, which included the potter's field. Potter's fields are graveyards for the indigent, the unclaimed dead, or those whose families couldn't afford or be bothered to bury them. These have often been impermanent places, abandoned after an epidemic, when full, or when the money for upkeep has run out.

The coroner's office had the records for the county cemetery piled up in a spare room, and with no time to deal with them, they were happy for my dad to take the files back to the library. While transcribing some of the hand-written cemetery records, he came across a 1957 Latter-Day Saints list of burials. "I became incensed when I found many of the names crossed through in pencil, and the word 'colored' replacing it," my dad said. I, too, was troubled by the injustice, the erasing of people's names, and the seeming lack of dignity given to those buried in mass graves.

I had lived in Boston for a decade by this time, and while I was in Fresno visiting my parents for a couple weeks, I asked to come along on one of my dad's graveyard outings. We would visit family member's graves, but I was also very curious to see what a potter's field looked like. I'd never before heard of a potter's field. I'd never considered what happened after death to the numerous homeless people I passed on the streets.

After taking the pictures of my great-grandparent's grave

markers, we walked toward the back of the cemetery, beyond an elaborately decorated building, with its pillars and marbled walls. This ornate structure held cremation lots. As we walked on, I wondered if that was where the phrase, "one's lot in life" had come from. When we reached the chain-link fence that bordered the cemetery, my dad pointed past it towards a mess of weeds. "I don't think we can get in, but that's it." I peered through the holes in the fence, amazed that what we were looking at adjacent to the lush green lawns of Holy Cross Cemetery was also considered a cemetery. It was a barren lot lacking any grave markers or other indicators that it was a place of burial. Anyone could drive right by and all they'd see would be an empty dirt field with a handful of mare's tails in one corner. Mare's tails are notoriously nasty weeds. Weed killer has little effect so they have to be pulled out by their roots. These plants stand three feet tall, are thin in stature, and have needles for leaves. They look like nature's toilet scrub brushes.[1]

As I processed the views of this neglected lot, I struggled for words and meaning. I wondered how many times throughout my life I had driven past here to go to the nearby Catholic cemeteries

---

1. Horsetail (*Equisetum arvense*), often called mare's tail, is an invasive, deep-rooted perennial weed that will spread quickly to form a dense carpet of foliage, crowding out less vigorous plants in beds and borders. They affect areas such as, beds, borders, lawns, paths, and patios. They usually arrive via rhizomes from neighboring gardens or from fragments of compost and manure. They're seen most often in spring and late summer.

where my grandparents and great-grandparents were buried, or to go to the zoo or the Roeding Park Playland. It was an empty field, land without a purpose, not land that held the bodies of thousands. My attention rested on the weeds, and all that came to mind was the old cliché, *pushing up daisies*, or in this case pushing up mare's tails.

The barren dirt field next to the weedy area was actually the cemetery grounds of the Chinese-American Society. A 2015 article from the local Fox News station, "Resting in Weeds," shed light on the mare's tail problem, focusing on the removal of these weeds in the Chinese-American cemetery, but failed to make any mention of the potter's field next to it. In the article was a quote in response to the weed-ravaged plots: "I would never let my family rest like that." But someone's family was resting like that: unseen and unremarkable. The potter's fields belonged to the county, so the Chinese-American Society had no obligation to remove the weeds in that section. The county did occasionally come out and weed, but it was an expense, and so not a regular occurrence.

I leaned closer into the fence and noticed small, unassuming numbers engraved in the thin stone strips that ran along the field every foot or so, like lines on a sheet of paper. My dad explained that these cement strips had plot numbers etched into them indicating where the graves were. The county used to bury only one person per plot, but they long ago ran out of room, so when that happened they began cremating everyone and burying 450 people per grave. I pictured a dry mix of cremated remains being dumped into a coffin. Dust to dust. In actuality, Fresno placed cremains in individual boxes with identification on them of who the person had once been. Boxes were cataloged in a database, and then put into storage. Once the county reached 450 people who had been cremated, boxed, recorded, and stored, they would open a plot and bury them together.

It seemed crass to be burying so many cremains in one grave: Boxed up, filed away, then buried in a mass grave with hundreds of others. Left for eternity to push up mare's tails, or at least until some county worker gets consigned to the thankless job of weeding. What I discovered upon telling and retelling this story of my experience with the potter's fields was that I wasn't alone in my ignorance. Whenever I told people about "potter's fields", I often received blank stares, which I'd then have to follow with some explanation. Others had knowledge of what they were but thought that they were an outdated concept.

After that first visit to the Fresno County Cemetery, I couldn't stop thinking about it. Each year after, when I'd come home for a visit, I felt the pull to return, just as I did other places that held importance for me. Instead of peering through the fence from the sanctuary of Holy Cross Cemetery, as we had the first time, we eventually found out how to enter the potter's field, where we could walk amongst the weeds, the coyote holes, the ever-deteriorating Chinese cemetery and headstones, the piles of trash that people had dumped (which my dad would call to have removed), and the occasional piles of plastic flowers, flags, dolls, religious figurines, and candles, that people had brought to pay their respects.

In doing so, we discovered one headstone in the potter's field, which we would later discover was created in the early nineties by a funeral director, Jim Copner. Jim and his son made the headstone as a memorial for one of the mass burials for those who died between 1979 and 1989. In 1995, when the headstone was placed during a service for those being buried, the local newspaper, *The Fresno Bee*, covered the event and interviewed eighteen-year-old Eustolia Ramirez who was there to remember her mother, Julia Chavez. Julia had died when Eustolia was five. The family didn't have money to cover the burial costs, so her mother became one of the 450 buried that day in Row 37, Section S, Grave No. 53.

Dignity Isn't Free

By 2018, the mare's tails were gone, perhaps removed in preparation for the service, and the flurry of activity as everything was put into place for the ceremony made for a party-like atmosphere. All the big Fresno news outlets were there. Yet, in the midst of the commotion, it was hard to miss the men working with the backhoe and shovel. We were surprised that the holes were just being dug. But after walking up to the two plots it was evident that we weren't going to see the burial actually happen. They had already dug the holes, buried the coffins with the cremains and filled it back in — they were merely bringing extra dirt to smooth over the top.

Awnings were set up with white plastic chairs placed beneath them, and a podium was carried by a couple of workers. One man handed out programs: on the front of the 6" x 9" folded cardstock was an angled image of an unidentified nature scene, with tall blades of bright-green grass creeping up from the bottom of the page dotted with red and yellow flowers, a few tree branches leaning in from the left side. Set behind the grass and trees was a river undulating past.

Where was this scene meant to be? If I hadn't been standing in the vacant dirt lot that was Fresno County Cemetery, or hadn't known the reality of the landscape of Fresno as hot dry desert,

I might have thought, *What a nice, comforting picture.* It was an image of serenity. It was a lie. One woman, whose brother almost ended up in the mass burial that day, was quoted by the news as saying, "It's terrible…we have a pet cemetery that is prettier than this."

She wasn't wrong.

Underneath the awning where I stood, was a patch of green turf that had been laid down with plastic folding chairs placed on top of it for any mourners who wanted or needed a seat. At some funerals, there is green turf that cemeteries use to lay over the mounds of dirt for families who prefer not to see the land in its raw form. Sometimes this is too much of a reminder that their loved one is dead. Too much of a reminder that they're burying their dad/brother/wife/daughter within that dirt. Too much of a reminder that the earth is claiming them. Too evocative of the reality of decomposition and decay. As we waited for the service to begin, I watched a county worker set up one of two large flower arrangements with white roses and a bow, and behind him another worker walked past, shovel in hand, his helmeted head bent down past a stone wall with razor wire spiraled across the top.

A few days before the ceremony, Fresno County Cemetery had been home to an unhoused man, which wasn't uncommon. But the sheriff's department came through and physically removed him along with his things, in order to prepare for the upcoming burial and memorial service of nearly eight hundred indigent individuals, some of whom, like him, may have been unhoused when they died. That he was cleared out so the rest of us could come and pay our respects to those like him felt wrong, hypocritical. Would it be too stark a reminder of how as a society we have failed too many to actually see an embodiment of who we were memorializing? Many of those buried that day may not have been homeless, but were living in that tenuous margin of being too poor to have any agency in where and how they were buried.

Dignity isn't free.

The path that leads someone to a potter's field as their final resting place is a complex, layered, messy one. Actually, there isn't just one path, but many, which often begin long before the death bed, that may lead to the same dismal end. A few years earlier, in 2015, a woman appeared around the corner from my parents' house, the woman stood on the sidewalk adjacent to a neighbor's backyard fence. A shopping cart, full of her things, was parked on the street curb nearby. She stood there for three days. During that time, my mom periodically went out for walks to confirm whether she was still there. It was the fall of 2015, and I was staying with my parents while I taught a semester at a local community college. One afternoon, as I drove past the corner near where this woman stood, I wondered why she'd chosen that spot. It seemed that she might have been trying to obey city loitering laws to avoid getting moved along; she was in a residential area, not in front of any shop, and she was on the side of the house, so out of view from windows and not obstructing doorways or walkways. As a woman, I could also imagine that it might be a safer option than others. If she were to be attacked there, possibly people would hear her screams in a quiet neighborhood at night, someone might notice a struggle and be able to intervene. It was also notable that she never sat while she was there. Someone once told me that this was because if she didn't lean or sit, the police couldn't make her move, yet I was unable to verify whether this was an actual law on the books in Fresno at the time. For those three days, she remained on that sidewalk corner, minus any time, I have to assume, when she may have left to go sit down for a bit, sleep, piss, shit, and generally be a living person. Why she decided to move when she did, I can only guess. It certainly wasn't a permanent solution of any kind, but maybe she'd found somewhere better to go, maybe someone finally came along and asked her to move, or perhaps she just decided to give up her position as living statue, the endless standing becoming too much.

Growing up in Fresno during the 1980s and 1990s, I don't recall homelessness being the ubiquitous thing it is now. One obvious reason for this is that it wasn't until the 1980s that the United States really saw a substantial jump in homelessness. At this time shrinking economic opportunities coincided with decreased safety-net protections (Padgett et al. 3). Bigger cities were hit the hardest. It wasn't until 2004, when homeless encampments in Fresno, such as Tent City (located on the West side of town under Highway 180) started gaining traction, which was a few years after I'd moved away to Boston. The Poverello House (a homeless service charity in Fresno) upgraded tents that sat on wood pallets, which they'd been using for temporary housing, by moving people into a neighborhood of individual-size toolsheds that they named the Village of Hope (Rhodes). Yet hope wasn't enough, and soon after the 2008 recession, things got worse. With five thousand people calling Tent City home by 2013, it had grown large enough to draw attention from academics who wrote theses on it (Speer) and journalists from news outlets and publications, including NPR and GQ, who came to write articles on its inhabitants and their lives there.

This is when Fresno officially disbanded Tent City, possibly due to some of the attention it had received, requiring the encampment's residents to find other places to shelter throughout the city. With few options, some like the woman on the corner near my parents' house, moved north into various residential neighborhoods. Many found their way to the live on along the banks of the myriad of irrigation canals that snake their way through Fresno. Others wound up breaking into abandoned homes in West or Central Fresno, a leftover consequence of the 2008 housing market collapse. Sometimes the illegal inhabitants of these abandoned homes would accidentally start fires, often in an effort to keep warm, have light, or to cook with, and sometimes those fires would get out of control and burn the houses down.

For years, each morning my dad has awoken before sunrise and walked four miles along the embankments of the canals, one of which passes right behind their home. On that same visit home, I decided to accompany him one morning, which was how I found myself walking in semidarkness at 5:00 a.m. along the canal. My dad carried a walking stick with him, not for support but to beat away one of the many packs of stray dogs that might pass by him and become aggressive. Only a few minutes into our walk, and just houses down from my parents' place, the dark air began mingling with a stringent, toxic smell. I put my hand to my face to try to protect myself from the burning I felt in my nostrils.

"The neighbor's burning trash again," my dad replied to my actions and the horrified look on my face. I responded with shouting about how disgusting that was and he quickly shushed me, not wanting to draw attention from the people doing the trash burning. As we moved farther along, we passed by large piles of garbage, and on the end of one pile sat a man surrounded by his belongings. When I first saw him, I thought he was a child's doll—moonlight hitting a porcelain face staring out from a sleeping bag—but as I stared back, the eyes blinked.

By this point, people in Fresno were calling for something to be done about the rise in homelessness. But the reality was less about a large spike in numbers and more about a slight growth in numbers combined with the displacement of the people who'd previously resided in Tent City and other encampments who now were living unhoused directly alongside the housed. As my dad and I returned home that morning, I was grateful for the sun rising and to no longer be out on the canal banks in the dark. It seemed to me that the homeless were the least scary thing we'd encountered on our walk compared to the person illicitly burning trash in their yard and polluting the air with toxins, the threat of stray dog attacks and piles of dangerous garbage mostly being dumped by homeowners in the area. Yet none of those things seemed to arouse as much passion, or bring out the pitchforks, quite like the threat of the homeless "infestation." In Fresno, as with many other places, the fight over public space was beginning to heat up.

Right of Access: Private Property – Get Off My Lawn

Who has the right to exist, to be visible, in public spaces? This is a question that Boston has been negotiating in regards to the Boston Common since its inception. The Common is the oldest public park in the US. Established in 1634, it's been used for grazing livestock; Puritanical punishments, including a whipping post, pillory, and stocks; hanging people; a redcoat encampment during the Revolutionary War; public oratory, discourse, and public gatherings, including a rally led by Martin Luther King Jr.; protests against the Vietnam War; the 2017 Women's March; general entertainment and recreation, including picnics, walks, sitting on park benches, and tai chi; and more organized activities such as baseball games in summer and ice-skating on Frog Pond in winter.

The Freedom Trail Foundation, a tourist website, notes, "Boston Common is open for all to enjoy." But this was not so. When I volunteered at the foot care clinic in Boston, one man told me how the city was clearing out the homeless for the summer by making sleeping in the Boston Common park a fineable offense so that tourists wouldn't see them. He went on to claim that the government was responsible for all the opioid deaths inflicting swaths of the homeless population across the country. His gaze bore into mine as he spoke. "How else do you explain how fentanyl so quickly replaced heroin, huh? They're trying to get rid of us." It would come out a few years later that much of the opioid crisis was tied to the pharmaceutical industry's push for profit amid a display of capitalism at its finest. Of course, there wasn't any covert operation by the US government to kill off the homeless, but he wasn't wrong in that they did want them out of sight.

Between 2010 and 2020, it seems that as homelessness grew, or at least became more visible, the fight over public space intensified in cities all across the United States and the world:

- In San Francisco in 2019, residents of the Mission District paid for and installed twelve large boulders on the sidewalks in their neighborhood to deter "what they described as a year of flagrant drug-dealing and unpredictable behavior. Housing advocates and other civically minded critics were quick to call the boulders out as anti-homeless architecture" (Ho).

- In 2017, Fresno passed the Unhealthy and Hazardous Camping Act in 2017 in response to the rising voices demanding something be done about the visible homeless problem. This made camping in tents or lean-to shelters on both public and private property illegal across Fresno.

• In Hungary, a social affairs state secretary bluntly stated that legislation in the form of anti-homelessness laws seemed to be designed to dictate use of space for the homeless versus the citizen. In other words, if one is homeless, then for all intents and purposes they are considered stateless noncitizens.

When calls for reducing homelessness and political war-waging over public access reach a crescendo, as they have in recent years, the government seems to have two primary tools for dealing with it: sequestration/corralling or criminalization. Either cordon off the offending groups or try to police their way out of the problem, with visibility at the core of both options. In one photo I came across, a man stands alongside a tent beside the fence of an abandoned property with a handwritten sign that reads, "If not here, then where?" (Policy Advocacy Clinic)

Modern Day Hoovervilles

In 1939, John Steinbeck wrote in The Grapes of Wrath:

And then the raids—the swoop of armed deputies on the squatters' camps. Get out. Department of Health orders. This camp is a menace to health

Where we gonna go?

That's none of our business. We got orders to get you out

of here…[and] the tractors moved in and pushed the

tenants out…

In spite of all these state and federal rulings, the reality is much more complex, and regular sequestration and criminalization of unhoused people still occurs. With regard to that first option—corralling and sequestering groups of people experiencing chronic homelessness—tent cities are the most obvious way of doing this. Usually set in parts of town where there's little commerce and therefore not much public activity, these locations can be out of sight and out of mind. An NPR article notes how the growing encampments in California "evoke shantytown 'Hoovervilles,' where hundreds of thousands of destitute Americans lived during the Great Depression. The encampments are…fueling a debate over poverty and inequality in one of the nation's wealthiest states" (Westervelt).

One of the most infamous encampments is Skid Row in Los Angeles, California. As *Los Angeles Times* reporter Steve Lopez notes of Skid Row, "[it] smells like the death of hope" (Dateline). But for decades now, Los Angeles has tolerated Skid Row's existence because its fifty square blocks have acted as a sort of barrier, penning in and containing a large mass of people in homelessness. But as the homeless crisis and the number of people on the streets grew in California, the borders of places like Skid Row began to creep out or dissolve completely. There wasn't enough space for everyone, and the poorest of the poor began to comingle with the richest of the rich, resulting in conflict. Venice Beach, an exclusive neighborhood in Los Angeles, is one battle site where people who live there have fought over the public spaces with those who are homeless and who are also using those spaces. In response to these issues, Los Angeles residents voted to increase their taxes to raise money for affordable housing. Yet when the city tried to use the money to build the affordable housing, neighborhood after neighborhood fought against it being built near them (Dateline). As encampments grow too large and spill into actively used space, such as shopping and business districts or residential neighborhoods, as seen with Skid Row and Tent City, the homeless are no longer seen as being successfully corralled. But being segregated to certain areas of town can produce unwanted consequences for those experiencing chronic homelessness, whether in shelters or encampments. Shelters and affordable housing are also often only allowed and placed in lower-income areas or on the outskirts of town, making them inconvenient for accessing necessary social and health services, and they are often too far away to commute for work.

I'm struck by how loud what isn't being said can be heard, like a dog whistle of mutual exclusivity being sung: us versus them, quality versus mediocrity, morality versus immorality, citizen versus homeless person. Without affordable housing, homeless encampments can sometimes be the safest and most preferred place of shelter for some. They don't operate under the same auspices of governmental control that shelters might, which means there's potential for more drug use and criminal activity. Yet on the flip side, it also means that people have the opportunity to govern themselves, they can better create trusted communities, maintain some semblance of control over how they live, and possibly avoid or reduce their level of institutionalization.

As anthropologist Robert Desjarlais writes in his 1997 book, *Shelter Blues: Sanity and Selfhood Among the Homeless*:

> The homeless can be felt too much. Those living on the streets and in shelters are disturbing because they threaten assumed paradigms of meaning…It is thus fitting that… shelters [be] set up … out of sight and beyond the reach of most social and economic commerce…[And] the most valued sites are policed in such a way that the poor and

others are forcefully kept away. We maintain and control the resources, the knowledge, the means of production and visibility.

Criminalization of poor and homeless people is not a modern invention. Under the guise of quality-of-life laws, the homeless are pushed out and driven away. This practice stems from a long history of sweeping the undesirable along. The United Kingdom's 1824 Vagrancy Act states that "…every person wandering abroad and lodging in any barn or outhouse, or in any deserted or unoccupied building, or in the open air, or under a tent, or in any cart or wagon, [not having any visible means of subsistence] and not giving a good account of himself or herself…" (The National Archives). American colonists developed vagrancy laws, which stemmed from the English Poor Laws. Coming into the nineteenth century, some cities and states created "ugly laws" that tried to ban people who were diseased, deformed, maimed, or mutilated. In the late 1800s, there were "sundown towns" in the Southern United States that banned African Americans from being out on the streets after dark. Cities in California did the same to Mexicans, Native Americans, and Chinese Americans. After the Dust Bowl and Great Depression drove people into California looking for work, California tried to outlaw these "Okies" from coming into the state

(Policy Advocacy Clinic).

As instances across the world, particularly in California, have shown, finding a solution to homeless encampments and their visibility is desired, but many don't want that solution to land in their proverbial backyards. When people have nowhere to sleep, sit, or perform basic bodily functions privately, they are forced to do these things in public spaces meant to be shared with all in the community. They're then penalized through citations, jailing, and other means that push them further into the system in ways that only perpetuate their state of homelessness and poverty, and the cycle repeats. Is the "choice" to live in a tent under a highway or on a canal really a choice?

Public health concerns do exist and need to be taken into consideration, but that means public health for everyone. Community members cite fears over fire risk, violence, and disease (Barry-Jester), yet often the ones most at risk are those in the camps. Although encampments are not up to public health standards, the consequences of being moved on without being placed in housing are also very serious. Numerous studies and organizations have shown that each time someone is moved from an encampment, they run the risk of losing so much:

Personal property,

medications,

identification,

shoes,

medical and legal documents,

blankets,

tents,

family photos,

… any sense of stability and safety.

These are things that hold meaning, tools to survive, small comforts, all being expeditiously gathered. People take what they can before the highway crews come through to clear out the area, what the campers in this area refer to as the Caltrans shuffle (Barry-Jester). It can be difficult, if not impossible, to imagine what it must feel like to frantically have to pack and move everything you own every few days or weeks. What's not difficult to understand, though, is how in the midst of such moves, crucial items, such as walkers, identification cards, and prescriptions, are lost and how devastating that could be (Herring).

Each time someone is cited for not moving on or for some other activity that falls within the purview of anti-homelessness laws, this creates a knock-on effect of misery and frustration:

A fine is issued that they can't afford to pay→ a bench

warrant is issued→ with no fixed address, they may miss any notices to appear in court and hearing dates → they get arrested→ miss crucial appointments necessary to receiving benefits → the likelihood of remaining on the streets increases, as well as engendering a further distrust of and disenfranchisement from the system. (Barry-Jester, Desjarlais, Herring, Hodge et al., Padgett et al., National Coalition of Homelessness).

Often when sanitation crews come through, people are prevented from collecting any of the belongings of those who aren't there at the time, which means that people are sometimes too afraid to leave camp, resulting in many unintended consequences. Sociologist, Chris Herring provides a haunting scene in his 2019 article, "Complaint-Oriented Policing: Regulating Homelessness in Public Space," that exemplifies such consequences:

> The threat of property destruction [and loss] resulted in homeless people avoiding the hospital, missing social service appointments, and being unable to hold a job…One of the elderly men who lost his property while hospitalized had called my cell phone before calling 911, as he lay paralyzed on a city sidewalk during a stroke, in hopes I could get to camp to watch his property before he was taken to the ER.

Who is Grievable?

Historically, across the centuries and the world, people have been and will continue to be buried in mass graves. Some lost to epidemic or natural disaster, others to the horrors of war or the evils of mass murders in the name of politics or ethnic cleansing. In the blog post, "Precariousness and Grievability - When is Life Grievable?" Judith Butler writes, "Only under conditions in which the loss would matter does the value of the life appear. Thus, grievability is a presupposition for the life that matters."

We grieve people who fought and died in wars, and those who died from famine, disease, or tragedy. We grieve them because we believe their lives had value and we may see them as brave or as victims of evil. We make the moral judgment that they were not perpetrators of their own demise, and therefore are worthy of our grief.

There are military cemeteries and war memorials dedicated to those who have died in battle. There are the locations of horrific tragedy and violence that become museums and sites of pilgrimage and tourism: the concentration camps of Germany and Austria, the Hiroshima Peace Memorial Museum. We name to remember, and in instances where we don't have names we have something like the Tomb of the Unknown Soldier, an important stand-in for soldiers whose bodies may have never been identified or found, for soldiers who never made it home.

In the United States, individuality is revered. It's a nation born of rugged individualism, inextricably linked to our personhoods, to our identities. In such a society, not being named is shameful. Dying anonymous becomes not so much a choice, as much as a social stigma for having been connected to a life seen as *less than*. So, I began transcribing names off headstones in the potter's fields I visited. Names that were already there for people to see. Yet, knowing that not many people came to visit, let alone knew of their existence, I felt a pull to type up as many of them as I could, to try and further memorialize them. Maybe someday others would see these names, read them, speak them aloud.

Each year in the United States, the names of all 2,753 people killed in the 9/11 attacks are read off in totality surrounded by the memorial, which has the names of every victim etched into the panels surrounding the reflecting pools that now stand where both towers of the World Trade Center once stood. It's painful, it's beautiful, it's necessary.

That day in Fresno during the mass burial to memorialize almost eight hundred people who had died in poverty, homelessness, or without friends or family, both the Catholic priest and the Unitarian minister spoke of naming. The priest impressing on us that God would remember the names of those we didn't know in life. The minister recited a poem,

"A great poet once wrote[2],

Each of us has a name given by the source of life, and given by our parents.

Each of us has a name given by our stature and given by our smile.

Each of us has a name given by the mountains and given by our walls.

Each of us has a name given by the stars and given by our neighbors.

Each of us has a name given by our wrongdoing and given by our longing.

Each of us has a name given by our enemies and given by our love.

Each of us has a name given by our celebration and given by our work.

Each of us has a name given by the seasons and given by our blindness.

Each of us has a name given by the sea and given by our death.

2. Israeli poet Zelda.

The Unitarian minister finished his sermon by assuring us that the sheriff had documented the names of those being buried. Yet, no names would be read nor printed on the program that day. Did those being buried not deserve to have their names seen and heard?

It would have taken too long. People are busy.

The Space that Remains

We change the physical space through which we move via the erection or eradication of barriers. Fences that keep people out, sidewalks and crosswalks that keep pedestrians contained, large pieces of concrete placed strategically in front of buildings to keep cars from being driven into them, laws saying where your body can exist. Where do we have the right to be? Where do we belong? We alter spaces, but they also alter us. They shape our behavior as well as how we see ourselves and one another. The more spaces someone is barred from existing in, the more marginalized their existence becomes. Even spaces that they aren't explicitly barred from going into, such as a coffee shop, they may self-police and not go in out of discomfort and fear of being othered. When someone is unhoused, in addition to the daily business of surviving, they are also constantly negotiating space.

Perhaps the public witnessing of such injustice and inhuman living quarters regularly is the necessary impetus for communities and leadership to start actively exploring how homelessness can be solved instead of merely hidden. Time and again, it seems that when those experiencing homelessness are seen, it is only in the form of a blight: something to be weeded out so as not to dirty up the nicer parts of town. All this warring over space leads to social injustice in the form of economic and health disparities. Many who are homeless have the tri-morbidity of poor physical and mental health and drug or alcohol dependence, which may lead them down a path where, even in death, as is evidenced by the potter's field, they are forced to the far reaches of "wasted" space: the only space that remains.

As my dad left the cemetery after the mass burial on that hot September day, we dragged the bottoms of our shoes along the dirt-paved road trying to get out all the burrs stuck to the soles. We were quiet, our spirits low. We both agreed that a lackluster service was better than no service, yet something about it had left me feeling hollow and a little gross. It had felt disingenuous in a perfunctory sort of way. Yet, while the service conducted in Fresno seemed rather lacking, the sheriff's department had meticulously documented all the names, ages, and dates of birth and death that they had for each individual, along with the location/plot where they were interred that day in Fresno: something that hadn't always happened in the past.

Perhaps my feelings were rooted internally. I didn't want to be a tourist. I didn't want to be a gawker, who could tick the box of "concerned citizen" with minimal effort made. I wanted to be a witness to something powerful, but this made me realize that what I also wanted was to have a larger part in working towards a solution that afforded dignity to all.

When we got to the car, I took my black flats off and tipped them upside down, watching the sand pour out of them. A crescent-shaped layer of dirt had caked onto the tops of my feet, which carried the stark reminder of disparity between the rich and poor, the beloved and the forgotten. The potter's field had no tree-lined paved roads winding through avenues that housed gothic reminders of opulence, no perfectly manicured lawns with benches to sit and contemplate loved ones gone. Once the circus of today died down, the party disbanded and each of us home, all that would remain would be a dirt field, scored with strips of cement with numbers etched in. Trash would be dumped; someone might bed down here for a night, a week, or longer; coyotes would come back and re-dig their holes. Mare's tails would grow once more, standing tall to watch over those who rested in this place.

Notes

A Certain Kind of Death. Directed by Grover Babcock and Blue Hadaegh, performances by Fred Corral and Sherwood Dixon, New Box Media, 2003.

Andrzejewski, Adam. "Mapping San Francisco's Human Waste Challenge—132,562 Cases Reported in the Public Way Since 2008." *Forbes,* 15 Apr. 2019. www.forbes.com/sites/adamandrzejewski/2019/04/15/mapping-san-franciscos-human-waste-challenge-132562-case-reports-since-2008/.

Appleton, Rory. "Aggressive Panhandler Cited for 11th Time in 2016, Found with $1,800 in His Pocket." *The Fresno Bee*, 18 Jan. 2016, www.fresnobee.com/news/local/crime/article55370835.html.

Barry-Jester, Anna Maria. "Sweeps of Homeless Camps in California Aggravate Key Health Issues." *NPR*, 10 Jan. 2020. www.npr.org/sections/health-shots/2020/01/10/794616155/sweeps-of-homeless-camps-in-california-aggravate-key-health-issues.

Borba, Jeanie. "Gathering to Remember: Burying the Grief of so Many Years." *The Fresno Bee*, 22 Sep. 1995.

"Boston Common." *The Freedom Trail Foundation*, www.thefreedomtrail.org/trail-sites/boston-common. Accessed 22 Mar. 2019.

Butler, Judith. "Precariousness and Grievability - When is Life Grievable?" *Verso Books*, 16 Nov. 2015, https://www.versobooks.com/blogs/2339-judith-butler-precariousness-and-grievability-when-is-life-grievable.

Calix, Brianna. "How Many People Are Homeless in Fresno and Madera? A Tally Happens This Week." *The Fresno Bee*, 23 Jan. 2018, www.fresnobee.com/news/local/article196063594.html.

---"'We Have to Do Better.' Will Fresno Finally Get a New Homeless Shelter?" *The Fresno Bee*, 21 Sep. 2018, www.fresnobee.com/latest-news/article218794730.html.

Cervantes, Raquel. "Blighted, Vacant Homes 'Magnets' for Fires." *Your Central Valley*, Jul. 2017, www.yourcentralvalley.com/news/local-news/blighted-vacant-homes-magnets-for-fires/128978033.

"Criminalization." *National Coalition for the Homeless*, www.nationalhomeless. org/issues/civil-rights/. Accessed 27 Feb. 2020.

Courtenay, Tamsen. *Four Feet Under: Thirty Untold Stories of Homelessness in London*. Unbound, 2018.

Desjarlais, Robert. *Shelter Blues: Sanity and Selfhood among the Homeless*. U of Pennsylvania P, 1997.

"Department of Transitional Assistance." *Commonwealth of Massachusetts*, www. mass.gov/eohhs/gov/departments/dta/. Accessed 5 Dec. 2019.

"Eighth Amendment: Excessive Fines, Cruel and Unusual Punishment." *National Constitution Center*, www.constitutioncenter.org/interactive-constitution/ amendment/amendment-viii. Accessed 15 Jan. 2020.

Extremis. Directed by Dan Krauss, performance by Jessica Zitter, Netflix, 2016.

Gee, Alastair. "At Night on Skid Row, Nearly 2,000 Homeless People Share Just Nine Toilets." The Guardian, 30 Jun. 2017, www.theguardian.com/us-news/2017/jun/30/la-skid-row-homeless-toilet-access-report.

Herring, Chris. "Complaint-Oriented Policing: Regulating Homelessness in Public Space." *American Sociological Review,* vol. 84, no. 5, 2017, pp. 769-800.

Ho, Vivian. "Blocked Sidewalks: How Boulders Became a Flashpoint in San Francisco's Homeless Crisis." *The Guardian*, 3 Oct. 2019, www. theguardian.com/us-news/2019/oct/02/san-francisco-boulder-homeless-crisis.

Hodge, James G., et al. "Homelessness and the Public's Health: Legal Responses." *Journal of Law, Medicine and Ethics,* vol. 45, no. 1, 2017, pp. 28-32.

KMPH. "Resting in Weeds: Problems in Keeping Up Fresno Chinese Cemetery." *KMPH*, 10 Jul. 2012, www.kmph.com/archive/resting-in-weeds-problems-in-keeping-up-fresno-chinese-cemetery.

Kushel, Margot. "How the Homeless Population Is Changing: It's Older and Sicker." *The Conversation*, 8 Jan. 2016, www.theconversation.com/how-the-homeless-population-is-changing-its-older-and-sicker-50632.

Kusmer, Kenneth, L. *Down and Out on the Road: The Homeless in American History.* Oxford UP, 2002.

Lea, Rachel. "'The Shitful Body': Excretion and control." Medische Antropologie, vol. 11, no. 1, 1999, pp. 7 – 18.

Legal Information Institute. "U.S. Constitution." *Cornell Law School*, www.law.cornell.edu/constitution. Accessed 5 Mar. 2020.

Magnatta, Marisa. "Someone Made an Interactive San Francisco Poop Map." *WMMR*, 17 Apr. 2019, wmmr.com/2019/04/17/someone-made-an-interactive-san-francisco-poop-map/.

Matlock, Kelly Anne. Interview. Conducted by Amy Shea, 12 Jan. 2015.

McCormick, Erin. "Big Brother on Wheels? Fired Security Robot Divides Local Homeless People." *The Guardian*, 17 Dec. 2017, www.theguardian.com/us-news/2017/dec/16/san-francisco-homeless-robot.

Mitchell, Don. "The Annihilation of Space by Law: The Roots and Implications of Anti-Homelessness Laws in the United States." *Antipode*, vol. 29, no. 3, 1997, pp. 303-35.

National Coalition for the Homeless. *Tent Cities in America: A Pacific Coast Report.* National Coalition for the Homeless, 2010.

National Law Center on Homelessness and Poverty. *Housing Not Handcuffs 2019: Ending the Criminalization of Homelessness in U.S. Cities.* National Law Center on Homelessness and Poverty, 2019.

Newsbeat. "Hungary Enforces 'Cruel' Ban on Rough Sleeping." *BBC News,* 15 Oct. 2018, www.bbc.com/news/newsbeat-45860488.

Oliviere, David, et al. *Death, Dying, and Social Differences.* Oxford UP, 2011.

Padgett, Deborah K., et al. *Housing First: Ending Homelessness, Transforming Systems, and Changing Lives.* Oxford UP, 2015.

Payne, Keith. "How Inequality Shortens Lifespan." *Literary Hub,* 5 May 2017, www.lithub.com/how-inequality-shortens-lifespans/.

Pidd, Helen. "Council Proposes £1,000 Fines for Homeless People Sleeping in Tents." *The Guardian,* 24 Nov. 2017, www.theguardian.com/society/2017/nov/24/council-proposes-1000-fines-for-homeless-sleeping-in-tents.

"Punishing the Poorest: How the Criminalization of Homelessness Perpetuates Poverty in San Francisco." *Coalition on Homelessness,* 18 Jun. 2015, http://www.cohsf.org/Punishing.pdf.

Rhodes, Mike. "Fresno Homeless Moved into Tool Sheds." Central Valley, 22 Nov. 2004, National Law Center on Homelessness and Poverty.

Saunders, George. "Tent City, U.S.A." GQ, 15 Sep. 2009, www.gq.com/story/homeless-tent-city-george-saunders-fresno.

Selbin, Jeffrey, et al. "California's New Vagrancy Laws: The Growing Enactment and Enforcement of Anti-Homeless Laws in the Golden State." *UC Berkley School of Law,* 12 Feb. 2015, www.homelesshub.ca/resource/californias-new-vagrancy-laws-growing-enactment-and-enforcement-anti-homeless-laws-golden.

Sheehan, Tim. "Ban on Homeless Camping Wins Fresno City Council Approval." *The Fresno Bee,* 17 Aug. 2017, www.fresnobee.com/news/local/article167906722.html.

Sibley, Gene. Interview. Conducted by Amy Shea, 2 Feb. 2020.

Siegler, Kirk. "Fresno Officials Dismantle Homeless Encampments." *NPR*, 26 Sep. 2013, www.npr.org/2013/09/26/226497851/fresno-officials-dismantle-homeless-encampments?t=1583416331652.

Slick, Matt. "Who Bought the Potter's Field, Judas or the Jews?" *Christian Apologetics and Research Ministry,* www.carm.org/bible-difficulties/potters-field. Accessed 1 Jul. 2020.

Sloane, David Charles. *The Last Great Necessity: Cemeteries in American History.* John Hopkins UP, 1991.

Song, John, et al. "Dying on the Streets: Homeless Persons' Concerns and Desires about End of Life Care." *Journal of General Internal Medicine,* vol. 22, no. 4, 2007, pp. 435-41.

Speer, Jessie. *Right to the Tent City: The Struggle over Urban Space in Fresno, California.* Syracuse University, Master's Thesis, 2014.

Steinbeck, John. T*he Grapes of Wrath.* Penguin, 1939.

"The City of Angels." *Dateline.* NBC, 19 Aug. 2018.

Tobias, Manuela, and Matt Levin. "California Just Counted Its Homeless—a Tally Sure to Be Inaccurate, and Politically Weaponized." *The Fresno Bee*, 30 Jan. 2020, www.fresnobee.com/news/local/article239607353.html.

"Vagrancy Act 1824." *The National Archives*, www.legislation.gov.uk/ukpga/Geo4/5/83/section/4. Accessed 22 Mar. 2019.

"Welcome to the Fresno County Sheriff's Office Website." *Fresno County Sheriff's Office*, www.fresnosheriff.org/. Accessed 24 Jul. 2020.

Westervelt, Eric. "Sprawling Homeless Camps—Modern 'Hoovervilles'—Vex California." NPR, 13 Jan. 2020, www.npr.org/2020/01/13/795439405/sprawling-homeless-camps-modern-hoovervilles-vex-california.

Wills, Garry. *Lincoln at Gettysburg: The Words That Remade America.* Simon and Schuster, 1992.

SHE WANTS TO LEAD

Ananda Lowe

H avana Club is a cavernous and windowless room, designed to make patrons of this popular dance venue forget about time as though they're in a Las Vegas casino. In the summers, the air conditioning and the industrial-size fans in the corners can't keep pace with the heat generated by three hundred gyrating bodies. Though I won't be in my forties much longer, on nights out my wardrobe comes from the juniors department: tight gold leggings, a black ruffled top, hoop earrings, and red velvet three-inch heels. (The blouse covers my belly at least; I count the number of revealing items I am wearing before leaving home, and limit it to three.) My Afro is extended to its limits, and my lipstick is the color of dark blood. You might not imagine the transformation that I make if you saw me during daytime hours.

*

Learning to dance as an adult can be thrilling, terrifying, or both.

Although I wasn't new to dancing, waking up on a sunny Sunday morning a couple of years ago, I was surprised to feel flooded by those emotions myself. They had to do with a series of dance classes that would begin that evening in Cambridge, Massachusetts.

Bachata is a style of dance from the Dominican Republic once regarded as low-class, "country" dancing; it recently experienced an explosion in international popularity thanks to a new generation of sexy young singers of the music. Today's stars are men like Romeo Santos, whose face looms over New York City on massive billboards, peddling songs that drip with sensuality, accompanied by blatantly R-rated music videos. (Of course, that's not unique to *bachata* music. Santos is first-generation American, and his video influences reflect that.) A loose, global network of dance instructors and performers capitalized on the music, gradually transforming the traditional footwork into a modernized style known as *bachata sensual,* Spanish pronunciation optional.

In the Cambridge/Boston area, right before pandemic times, over seventy Latin dance classes were offered weekly at homegrown dance schools, often immigrant-owned small businesses that crossed-over to a multiethnic clientele. During my decade in this community, I became comfortable with triple spins and cultivated the ability to be a gracious "follower" to men from around the world dancing in the role of "leader," with their ever-evolving dance steps.

When it is *bachata* night at the club, there is a difference in the air from salsa nights. Each song begins with the deep, rolling sound of an electric guitar, as if the instrument is licking its own lips in anticipation of what will come next. Dancers who may or may not know each other take on the characteristic intense embrace, where two bodies undulate as one. In the contemporary style, leaders and followers face each other and travel in unison, four steps to one side, then four steps to the other side. The movements can be compressed — so the couple is huddling in place and barely traveling — or they can be expanded, so that with the swoop of a leg across the floor, the couple's choreography occupies a space that's wider than they are tall. I once asked an Australian to dance me around an entire 2,000 square foot room packed with people — in one song — and he did. In salsa, the two dancers pass each other by in a tiny space, back and forth. But in *bachata*, they merge. Both dances are beautiful, but the latter can feel nearly intoxicating.

Years ago, I knew I was home when I found *bachata*.

*

To increase my skills, in July 2018 I enrolled in a new series of *bachata* classes at my favorite dance studio, Rumba Y Timbal in Cambridge. When I woke up that Sunday, my surprising first thought was: *Am I announcing something to the world about my sexual orientation by taking this class tonight?*

My plan was to take the class as a female lead — for the first time — in a dance form deeply rooted in a binary gender system. Latin dance styles are based on intricate Afro-Caribbean rhythms and body movements. These are melded with European elements such as the centuries-old custom of leading as "masculine" and following as "feminine," a tradition which is as beautiful and skillful as it is flawed. *Machismo* culture also has European origins. The question running through my mind, when expanded, would read: does the role in which someone dances indelibly confirm their gender? And as the transgender movement asks, is someone's gender expression equal to that person's sexuality?

For *bachateros* and *salseros* who began dancing in the past generation, the image of a woman who could lead was close to nonexistent. Aside from a few female instructors, for many years the only one I knew was Jonna Tufts, a dancer originally from

Bridgewater, Massachusetts. She learned to lead as a student of Erika de Leon at the Salsa Rosa Dance Academy while living in Quetzaltenango, Guatemala in 2004.

"I just really wanted to dance," she told me, "and didn't want to feel stuck without a male leader. When then music moved me, I couldn't stand to sit still."

Regarding male follows, there was a tiny handful of skilled guys who sometimes partnered with male leaders. It seemed to be an indication that they were totally badass dancers, or they were hipsters from New York City — not that they were gay, which the Latin dance community chose not to discuss. These men were hands-down my favorite dancers to watch at the clubs, because it took so much talent to dance in the "opposite" role, their dancing was gorgeously executed, and I found it completely hot.

I also found it a thrill to dance with Jonna as my leader. To be clear, I was in a serious romantic relationship with a man; I had long established my identity as a woman who would be happy to be in a monogamous relationship with either sex. I was in my thirties, and I wasn't hungry for sexual contact with anyone other than the mate I already had. When I danced with a female leader, or watched an amazing male follower on the dance floor, I found it sexy in the same way traditional male-female dance couples were sexy. Any two partners who could turn dancing into a visual art were exciting. The same-sex couplings added a subversive edge that provoked the brain by doing something which, at the time, was startlingly unexpected.

Just a couple of years ago, more women leads began stepping out onto nightclub floors. Since early on in my dance journey I'd wanted to do the same, but always came up with excuses not to. Then that summer, a new series was starting at the dance school in Cambridge. The beloved director of the school, Roberto Figueroa, was a former member of the El Salvadoran military whom I thought of as, well, macho and somewhat intimidating, but the best technical instructor around. The only class that fit into my schedule was Beginner *Bachata*, in which I could choose to learn to lead.

When I was a teenager, my family had not been able to accept me and my sexuality. The loss, fear and rejection I felt never fully went away. Decades later, on the first day of *bachata* class in 2018, I wasn't expecting those to be my initial thoughts of the morning. But they were what I woke up to, and I felt uncontrollably panicked about facing the day.

*

Why did I wait more than ten years to learn to lead? For starters, we're a species that does as we're told.

Nationwide and until recently, nearly all ballroom, Latin, and partner dance instructors could be heard to say "men, do this; ladies, do that." The first time I heard anyone say otherwise was in 2017 when Eli "Lady" Pabon was teaching a large public salsa class outdoors in the South End neighborhood of Boston. She said "it doesn't matter what gender you are. If you want to lead, stand here, and if you want to follow, stand there." I was confused and didn't fully trust what I'd heard at first. Like others who've lived through an era of persecution, it was hard to actually let myself feel safe.

When we learn to dance as adults, we're usually in a heightened emotional state. We're excited to inhabit our bodies if we've been out of touch with them for a while. We're hoping not to make total fools of ourselves. Huge numbers of people feel they require an alcoholic beverage before being relaxed enough to get onto a dance floor. When an instructor tells us what to do according to our gender, we're so wound up about everything else that it doesn't occur to most of us to question the logic of it. And then we spend years perpetuating a culture where only men lead... and what men are *only allowed* to do is lead.

And where women, of course, do the opposite.

Even in today's world, giving up gender roles means unraveling years of conditioning. Tanya Karen is a dancer who has described her "experiment" during visits to *bachata* dances in Berlin and London, in which she explicitly asked all potential male dance partners whether they would prefer to lead or follow.

"Every so often, I wonder what I'm doing dancing," she said. "I experience so many outdated gender norms and often feel objectified."

Her experiment produced a number of awkward moments for her and her dance partners, but she says it was worth it. "Because when men said 'yes' [to breaking norms] in this experiment, I finally felt like I belonged on the dance floor."[1]

*

On my first day of *bachata*-as-leader, the instructor Liliana Jimenez called out, "Who's going to be leading?" so everyone could identify their options for choosing a partner.

The guys and I raised our hands, and the women looked around in the semi-panic of having to connect with someone on the dance floor for the first time. I started to walk toward one of the women, and then another. It genuinely felt like they couldn't see me — not that they were willfully ignoring me, but as though they didn't realize I'd been serious when I raised my hand to be a leader. They glanced around for the expected maleness of their potential

1. http://socialdancecommunity.com/what-i-learned-by-asking-men-if-they-want-to-lead-or-follow-bachata/

partners and looked straight through me.

Finally, I found myself holding hands with a cheerful, encouraging young lady named Jessica. Then I awkwardly tried to figure out where to fix my gaze.

Dancing with men, I normally look them in the eyes and smile widely. The majority of them glance around the room and don't make eye contact while dancing. Other women, however, are likely to do what I do, and stare back at my face. Maybe that's why guys have learned to look away, because now I see how intense it is to have a stranger suddenly locking eyes with you from a foot away. First I tried resting my eyes on Jessica's necklace, but that felt a little too close to staring at her chest. Next I tried focusing on her ear, and then her shoulder, while still feeling acutely aware of her beaming smile. I hope I don't seem rude by not meeting my follower's eyes, but there's no obvious comfortable place to look.

Female followers are well-aware of the large range of leading styles among men, from those who touch us so lightly that we're unable to tell what steps they're signaling, to men who nearly break our hands with their grasp, to those who get it deliciously just right. Now I would have the chance to experience things from the other side.

*

On a Tuesday, two nights after my first *bachata* leader class, I go to the club. As I settle into a seat, it dawns on me that Liliana told us we should practice in between classes or we wouldn't make progress. An irony of gendered partner dancing is that most of my acquaintances here are guys, since that's who I dance and therefore mainly interact with. I know a few women, but I don't see any here tonight that I've ever spoken to, and it doesn't occur to me to pick one at random to ask to dance. I spot Vladimir out of the corner of my eye. He's one of my current favorite dance partners, gruff and silly at the same time, with a highly precise dance style.

I hesitate. I will need to plow through a dozen people to get to Vladimir. He shifts in his seat and it looks like he's about to get up to ask someone else to dance. I seem to have missed my chance to dance to this song, and I feel disappointed. A couple minutes later I realize the song is a long one, and I glance over to his seat again. He's still there, and I could've asked him to dance after all. I've missed my chance twice in one song, and it comes to an end.

Surely Vladimir will take advantage of a new song starting, and he will ask someone near him to dance. When he doesn't after the first several bars of music play, I propel myself in his direction and stand facing him in a way that almost feels confrontational. I'm nervous. The expression on his face is inscrutable.

"Could I lead you?" I stammer. He hesitates, as he appears to digest a question he wasn't expecting.

"Of course," he says.

"Do you know how to follow?" I ask, once we're on the dance floor.

"Yes," he replies sternly. "I mean… a little."

Every sentence feels awkward and strained between us. I start to lead the basic *bachata* step from right to left, the opposite of what I'm used to. It only takes a few seconds though, for Vladimir to correct what I'm doing.

"You need to keep a stiff frame!" he bellows at me with a Slavic accent, from underneath his thick mustache. I stiffen up, but it feels like I'm arm-wrestling him with all my strength, which is a losing proposal.

Finally, when I'm about to collapse from the effort, I say meekly, "I feel like I have to push really hard to lead like this."

"No," he replies. "Don't push. Just lean with your whole body, this way."

"Like this?" I say helplessly, sure that I'm not going to be able to master Vladimir-style *bachata*.

"That's… fine," he says. I'm going to assume that "fine" means it will do, and I try to move on.

It's tempting to try to execute my new moves by counting the eight beats of the dance out loud, and trying to remember exactly where Liliana said to place my hands and feet. But the more I think and concentrate, the more slowly I recall what to do. I decide to have faith in my muscle memory instead. I move Vladimir through a series of left and right turns, then spin myself, as I willfully push the rational instructions out of my brain. It manages to work. He smiles, and a look of surprise appears on his face, which also has the effect of slowing down the flow of suggestions he has. I know a total of about five moves so far, and I use them up in time for the song to end.

"Thank you!" I practically yell as we finish.

"I'm happy to be your punching box anytime," he says.

"Punching bag," I correct his English with a laugh. He gave me a backhanded compliment, but that's typical of his style and I'm going to take him at face value. I'm excited that now I have at least one follower I can ask to dance whenever I'm at the club, because it feels like there's no model for how to do this as a female lead.

*

Later that month, I ask an unfamiliar woman to dance, and I invite a man I just met out to dinner, all in one night. I have never done either of those things before. I'm beginning to notice how issues of leading and following manifest in other areas of my life.

As a young girl, I was encouraged to lead in outward pursuits such as school, but there was very little talk about how to be healthily assertive in intimate relationships. When it came to romantic partners, I spent a lifetime being an object of pursuit or abandonment. In spite of the gains of feminism, it felt deeply unacceptable for me to be the one to get a relationship started, or to end it, and I couldn't see a way around this. Most of the time, it felt like relationships "happened to" me.

Often, my passivity (and, you might say, my inability to lead) has interfaced with my lovers' dominating personalities, with negative results. This was heavily modeled by my own parents. When we deny girls the skills to take the lead in our closest relationships, it isn't a small thing. In cases like mine, a personality can become stunted for a long time. After separating from my long-term partner a few years ago, my next relationship was with a *bachata* dancer whose demeaning behavior seemed normal (based on my lifelong patterns), and didn't set off alarm bells for me right away.

It's too soon to say whether becoming a dance lead will dramatically change the rest of my existence, but I am curious to find out. I'm not just learning to move my feet in reverse. As simple as it sounds, what I know so far is that I'm feeling a deep and newfound sense of my own capabilities.

And I'm wondering why this was kept from me all my life.

*

There's a difference, too, between leading a male or female dance partner. A person socialized as female brings qualities to the dynamic such as responsiveness, receptivity, eagerness to please, and self-blame when she makes a mistake. When I dance as a leader with men, I perceive something different. Men who are newer dancers, and don't yet have the body memory to be solid leaders, are often enthusiastic to experiment, seem relieved to give up control for once in their lives, and are willing to trust that I know what I'm doing.

On the other hand, experienced male leaders are in the position of going against their training when they follow, and they can be defensive about their mistakes rather than apologetic. I feel a greater need to be gentle with them or I fear they will quit after only a couple of moments (which has actually happened). One of my favorite male leaders tensed his forehead, and said in a plain and chilly voice when I asked to lead him, "I don't do that."

The best technique I've discovered so far is to simply start by leading a man in the "basic step," the eight-count from side to side, over and over before anything else happens. All other steps flow from that. You'd think the basic step would require the least practice, but I've found that the opposite is true to establish a secure foundation. (Maybe this approach can be applied to intimate relationships, too.)

*

When there's no pandemic, as a part-time job I take tourists to salsa and *bachata* clubs, usually first-time dancers. They come from many parts of the world, although some of them are local to Boston. We start by grabbing dinner at Zuzu restaurant, during which it's my job to calm their nerves and paint a mental image of the details involved in having a comfortable debut at a dance club. (For example, although they may feel anxious, I encourage them to line up in the front row of the dance lesson, under the spotlights, because it gives them the best view to learn the steps. I tell them how large the crowd will be, teach them how to ask others to dance, and hand out breath mints and earplugs.)

I only have a few minutes to explain gender roles in Latin dance to my guests. Here are some of the ways in which I've tried: "When you participate in the dance lesson, the old-fashioned approach is for men to be leaders and women to be followers. However, that's been changing in recent years, and you can take whichever role you choose."

A week later I've found myself saying, "You can choose to dance in any role that you'd like, but it's easier to learn if you take the traditional gender roles. That way, when the general dancing begins and people start asking others to dance, they will be able to tell which role you can dance by looking at you."

One of my guests responded by saying, "Really, why is that?"

"Because of your gender," her friend replied with a frown and eye-roll. "But when I took lessons from Liz Nania, she taught without being gendered about it."

She was referring to a local ballroom instructor who runs classes aimed at the LGBT community. A housemate of mine took classes from Liz for years. I was experimenting with ways to explain the shifting norms in dance to my tourist clients, but I felt that I was failing at figuring out how to do it without making someone uncomfortable.

The advertisement for my tourist events says "singles and couples of any orientation welcome." When a same-sex couple attends and wants to dance together, one of them will be required to take the "opposite" role. That usually goes smoothly enough. Interestingly, when male-female couples hear me say they can take any role, a number of them have excitedly decided they want to reverse roles. The vague idea of doing that appeals to them, even if they don't know what it means to lead or follow in any technical sense as a dancer. I think it's a great sign that not just a few outliers are interested in these options.

There's a dance pro at the club who leads a large group lesson. After the lesson, I continue teaching my guests one-on-one or in a smaller group. And although I can dance well as a follower and sufficiently as a leader, I don't yet have the mental bandwidth to teach a group where gender roles have been totally abandoned, without becoming confused myself.

Liz Nania, the LGBT dance instructor, has been teaching for more than two decades, along with hosting dance parties specifically for that community. But it's been barely a couple of years that members of the presumably straight Latin dance community have come out as LGBT, and begun the process of integrating the two communities.

The process is accelerating though, and faster than I would have expected. In Boston in 2017, an instructor named Tina Cavicchio went from having bra-length hair to a crew cut, and started using the word "queer" in the mainstream dance community. She doesn't see herself as an activist, just someone who leads by example (pun unintended). Her students adore her, and she creates integrated spaces simply by drawing people to her who feel safe around her, whatever their orientation. In 2018, the salsa icon Ana Masacote came out as part of the LGBT community in a Boston newspaper and on the radio, after maintaining an internationally-successful dance career for over fifteen years.

Just over a year before the pandemic, I started taking lessons as a beginning leader, then took a short break. When I came back to the next series of classes, I was now one of four female leaders, instead of the only one. Will we soon wind up with a completely gender-free Latin dance community? What would that be like? When women learn to lead in relationships, whether on the dance floor or at home, a source of power is unleashed in them. It is an incredible feeling. It would change not just how women feel about themselves as individuals, but also change the dynamics of the dance community.

I'm not saying everyone has to be bisexual and androgynous, free of gender or sexual preference altogether. (That should be one of the options.) Given the freedom, perhaps most members of society will stick with their traditional roles anyway. Even so, it should be voluntary, not enforced. When an entire gender feels that their only option is to be a follower in life, then we're all being stifled psychologically.

Some days, I'm bewildered to see the changes happening so rapidly. My friend Celia celebrated her birthday at Havana Club earlier this year, and there were so many women lined up to dance with her that her male friends stood aside, good-naturedly joking about not being able to dance with her. It feels like it happened in the blink of an eye, but it took a decade. In fact, it took more than a generation.

Having grown up in a harsher time, there's a part of me that's envious of people who are newly enjoying these freedoms without (I find myself assuming) having had to suffer. When election season rolls around, one of my family members reminds everyone that people died so that we could vote today. Lives were also lost on the road to embracing variations in gender and sexuality. This feels like a celebration I've been waiting for my whole life, yet it also can trigger a lifetime of painful memories. For me, there are moments when it feels like what I imagine revolution feels like — upheaval, joy, fear of the unknown, shock, destruction of the old, and sitting in the rubble while everyone laughs and cries all at once.

*

Back in 2016, I began dating a Latin dance-lover named Jaime. He held orthodox religious beliefs, and although he had a history of bisexuality, he felt guilty about having any kind of sex.

Nonetheless, we got along well for a while. During the early months of getting to know him, I was also getting reacquainted with the dance scene after a few years away.

One night we stood on the sidelines at the club, and two men danced skillfully together nearby, dazzling me as I remembered from a decade ago. I asked Jaime if he'd ever danced with male partners. "No way," he answered immediately. "I guess I'm not that secure in my sexuality."

"It's not a sign of sexual orientation," I said. "It means you're a badass and can do something really hard."

His eyebrow shot up and he pursed his mouth. "Um, that's not what I thought," he said, as our eyes met and we mulled each other's perspectives.

Maybe I'd thought the day would never come when people who were interested in the same sex romantically could express that on the dance floor, so I assumed it still wasn't the case.

As I began to witness some of the new developments in the Latin dance community, it dawned on me that both Jaime and I were correct. In the past, variations in gender and sexuality seemed completely invisible in Latin dance, while now they're sometimes on display. However, today it's just as possible that a group of straight sorority sisters are trying out the scene and having fun dancing with each other, or a man had a progressive dance instructor somewhere who asked students to learn the opposite role in order to master the craft. They might be women who began training in salsa or *bachata* during the last couple years and simply want to be able to dance with their female friends, never having known a time when it was practically unheard of. And, of course, it still could mean they're badass hipsters from New York City — the kind who couldn't care less about gender roles and won't let anything inhibit their joy of dance.

A Murmuration of Stones

Robbie Gamble

A plot. A boneyard. A potter's field. A necropolis. A golgatha.

I stumbled upon it one steamy day in the first summer of COVID, while my car was in the shop for repairs. Rather than hunker in a socially-distanced corner of the dealership waiting room while mechanics wrestled with a failed catalytic converter and timing belt, I decided to spend several hours wandering the drowsy streets of Waltham, a suburb just west of Boston. The sidewalks were deserted because of the heat, or the virus shutdown, or both, and I passed empty schoolyards, shuttered storefronts, dormant office parks, a winding succession of ranch and colonial homes; some rising pristine beyond manicured lawns, some peeling and overgrown, signaling despair.

On a whim, I cut through a stretch of wooded parkland, following a dirt track over a low ridge and down into a shady glen.

Around a bend, a peculiar stretch of shabby lawn came into view: long and narrow, like a landing strip hidden in the woods, bordered by a low stone wall. Each end of the clearing was studded with a grid of low granite blocks in orderly rows, and each weathered block was marked with a letter and a number crudely carved into its top face. A simple billboard mounted behind the stone wall proclaimed the clearing to be the Metfern Cemetery, where residents of the nearby Metropolitan State Hospital and the Fernald School were buried between 1947 and 1979. The sign noted that the letter "C" carved in the stones at the righthand end of the lot indicated Catholic burials, while the "P" markers at opposite end were for Protestant internments. That was it: no names, no circumstances, just a mute line of sentinel trees beyond the stone wall, and the dirt track winding its way back to meet up with Trapelo Road and the branching subdivision tracts inhabited by the living, sweltering residents of Waltham.

A scar on the earth. A minor state secret. A whiff of municipal shame. A murmuration of stones.

I vaguely remembered something about a reference to a Fernald School from a long-ago medical ethics class, a cringeworthy case of residential schoolboys fed radioactive oatmeal without their knowledge. I picked up my car and headed home to learn more about this secluded site and the institutions behind it. An internet search revealed that the Fernald School was originally named the Experimental School for Teaching and Training Idiotic Children when founded in 1848, and served as the primary state residential facility for well over a century, housing and training children with cognitive challenges on a campus of grim, red-brick institutional buildings. Many residents lived out their entire lives in spartan, 36-bed dormitories, and many reports of physical and sexual abuse have accumulated over the years. The state finally closed the campus in 2014, dispersing the final thirteen residents, one who had lived there for sixty-five years, into local community service programs, and selling the campus back to the City of Waltham, where it remains unused, a crumbling, brick-faced ghost town, propped up by its inclusion on the National Register of Historic Places.

The infamous radioactive oatmeal study that I had recalled was jointly sponsored by Harvard, MIT, and the Quaker Oats Company in the 1950's; boys were offered extra portions and trips to Red Sox games for participating in a "Science Club" where their nutritional uptake was assessed by tracking isotopes they ingested.

Neither the boys nor their parents were told of the nature of the study, or given adequate opportunity to provide informed consent for their participation. It took decades for the details of the project to come to light, and a class-action suit against MIT and Quaker finally resulted in a $1.85 million settlement for the surviving victims in 1998.

The Metropolitan State Hospital was Massachusetts' state-of-the-art public hospital for people with mental illness when it opened in 1930. At its peak in the 1950's, the hospital housed nearly two thousand patients, but Massachusetts joined up in the national trend toward deinstitutionalization of psychiatric patients, and in subsequent decades the Metropolitan's prestige and funding were gradually squeezed dry. The hospital closed in 1992, after an interminable bureaucratic struggle to arrange alternative housing and services for the last of the life-long residents being served there; its outbuildings were converted into condos and offices, and its central administration building, a hulking, Doric-columned massif in the Colonial Revival style, was also abandoned to the National Register of Historic Places, to be overrun with vines and graffiti.

Drilling deeper into the Metfern Cemetery story, I discovered a recent online project led by a Harvard Kennedy School faculty member, Alex Green, who enlisted a class of high school seniors to comb through state and town registries for birth, death, and immigration records, using these paper records along with online genealogy databases to build brief biographies of the 296 men and women they determined had been buried in the Waltham woods. The scraps they pieced together were threadbare: a birthplace, the names of parents or a spouse; sometimes an occupation, usually chronic medical and psychiatric conditions, and almost always a cause of death. Some of the residents in both institutions were forced to do hard menial labor, housework and groundskeeping, while others were too debilitated to work. The students built a public website where people can now linger over sketches of how these forgotten residents lived and died:

C-13: died of pneumonia 4/21/1949, age 83. C-59: diagnosed as having "idiocy", died 5/2/1958, age 80. C-34: born with hydrocephalus, died 6/24/1954, age 8 months. P-15: Born in Latvia, died of breast cancer 9/14/1949, age 63. C-116: fell out of wheelchair, lacerating his brain 8/12/1966, age 22. P-50: died of a heart attack while mowing the hospital lawn 5/16/1955, age 51.

One odd detail in the narrative of C-160 [died of pneumonia 12/12/1975, age 65] grabbed my attention: "at some point she had undergone a salpingectomy, in which the fallopian tubes are removed, and it does not appear that she had children." In such a scant rendering of a life, why do we learn that she was sterilized? And why go to the trouble to sterilize a childless woman, living in a secured institution? I learned the Fernald School was named after its third Superintendent, Walter Fernald, who had been widely lauded as an innovative early twentieth-century educator of "mentally retarded children." Fernald was also an ardent advocate for eugenics, the pseudoscience that posited one could improve the human race be carefully selecting who did and didn't pass along their genes by having children. American eugenicists feared that the country's potential talent and intelligence was at risk of being insidiously undermined by defective members of its lower classes. Involuntary sterilizations of women and men deemed hopeless alcoholics, "epileptics," "criminally insane," "feebleminded," and sexually promiscuous were common in state-run institutions around the country through the mid-twentieth century, and these procedures were practiced regularly at both the Fernald School and the Metropolitan State Hospital.

C-160's story cuts to my core because of the legacy of my grandfather, Clarence Gamble, who was an heir to an industrial fortune, a physician, a pioneer in the field of world population control, and a eugenicist. He lived in a white mansion on a hill south of Boston, and although he mainly focused his work in the developing world, he also promoted and funded sterilization programs in southern U.S. states, targeting mostly the rural poor, mostly people of color. He touted sterilization as a humane, inexpensive method for communities to control social costs by preventing new generations of hapless, *feebleminded* people from becoming expensive wards of the state, noting the procedures were barely invasive, just a snipping of tubes, and that "nothing needed to be taken out of the body." He often referred to his work as "The Great Cause," and I'm sure he approved of the efforts at Fernald and the Metropolitan in his own backyard, to stop people from passing on bad genes. I cringe when I consider his cause now, imagining a link in a long chain of elite initiatives, framed as medical progress, but built on the exploitation and suppression of the most marginalized humans among us:

J. Marion Sims, gynecological surgical experiments on enslaved women (1845). The Virginia State Colony for the Epileptics and Feebleminded (1910). Caswell Training School, North Carolina (1911). Buck v. Bell, Supreme Court ruling on sterilization (1927). The Tuskegee Syphilis Study (1932). Oral contraceptive clinical trials,

Puerto Rico (1956). Irwin County Detention Center, Georgia, coerced sterilizations of detained migrant women (2020).

I'm a nurse practitioner, and I've worked for twenty years with homeless people in Boston, accompanying folks through terrible crises and small victories in their difficult lives. I'm struck while reading the brief life sketches in the Metfern Cemetery project, that if these patients and residents were alive today, I might be caring for them in an outpatient clinic, helping to manage their blood pressure or HIV meds, accompanying them through relapses on booze and opiates, treating wounds after an assault or being hit by a car. I honestly don't know if they would be better off now, released from a lifetime of institutionalization in grim dormitories, instead living day-to-day in squalid shelters, or on the streets, catching a few hours' sleep on a subway bench or in an ATM booth. I do know this: with all the troubles they endure, they all have complex, valuable lives, and they each have stories to tell. In our clinics, when we learn someone has died, we share anecdotes about them, their quirks and passions, and we remember their names. And we hold an annual service to intone the names of those who died in the previous year in a litany, to hold them up in the light. Alex Green notes that there are countless internment plots and potter's fields like Metfern tucked into shady forgotten corners around the country. How consistently we ignore the most vulnerable in our midst, the living and the dead.

At least the numbered stones on this plot have reclaimed their names now:

C-13: John Edwin Higgins. C-59: Hannah "Anna" Berry. C-34: Diane Coleman. P-15: Mary Kivet. C-116: Vincent Strudas. P-50: Paul Werner. And C-160: Geraldine Etsell.

ON BEING (ASIAN)
Justin Chen

Reflections on Ambivalence and Identity

Sometime in early February of 2020, during the hazy weeks leading up to sheltering from home, I walked to the grocery store a few blocks from my apartment in Cambridge, Massachusetts. Despite reports of the virus overrunning cities in China and Italy, the pandemic seemed eerily distant from my immediate reality. In the store, people strolled casually down the aisles, occasionally bumping carts or brushing against each other. A couple in the produce section, framed by a misted array of peppers and broccoli, discussed an upcoming dinner party.

The only extraordinary detail was an Asian man in the checkout line. Wearing a blue, pleated surgical mask, he was the lone store-goer with a face covering. Like me, he appeared to be in his early thirties but his skittish politeness marked him as new to the country. Watching him nod to the cashier, I was overcome with revulsion, tenderness, and nostalgia.

Although I was raised by Taiwanese immigrants in the United States, I consider myself part of the prevailing culture — not *White* necessarily but comfortably mainstream. Growing up, I'd been aware of my Asianness but, until recently, I'd never thought deeply about my race or ethnicity. Within my middle-class life in a liberal city, I've floated through a frictionless and illusory world of equals.

Standing in line, behind the masked Asian man, my immediate desire was to distinguish myself from him — not only to the people around me but to myself as well. Even though we would all be wearing masks in another month, the man's precautions seemed overblown. "I'm not that kind of Asian," I wanted to declare to the rest of the store. In the man, I saw a reflection of my hesitant voice, flat face, and general otherness. The feeling was visceral but short lived and almost forgotten. Except that in the year since the start of the pandemic, the sensation has resurfaced with increasing complexity and contradictions.

The increased focus on anti-Asian racism during the Spring of 2021 made me more conscious of how others saw me and how I viewed myself. I began to feel both less and more Asian. While reading news stories of Asians being threatened, spit on, or assaulted, I'd experienced a detached anxiety; I thought about my parents or friends but not myself. Somehow, I didn't feel *Asian* enough to be in jeopardy. This dissociation was a way of downplaying danger but also, more insidiously, an attempt to Westernize myself by excluding my minority identity.

At the same time, it became more difficult, and ridiculous, to ignore how others perceived my Asianness. Every lingering or second glance from strangers while walking down the street seemed loaded with new weight and meaning: suspicion, fear, disgust, sympathy.

It feels strange to be Asian, more specifically Taiwanese, without speaking the language, eating national dishes, or celebrating holidays. Growing up in suburban New Jersey, my younger sister and I rarely spoke to our parents about their lives before they came to America. We were inculcated with the standard immigrant mythology of striving and sacrifice but learned little about where they had come from. Taiwanese culture was a mystery to me — an absence I felt but couldn't define. I was lonely for something without having the ability to describe what I was missing.

My few recollections of Taiwan, from occasional visits, are cloudy with romanticism: The lush island humidity, riding on the back of a bicycle with my cousin through the bustling streets of Taipei at night. Most of all, I remember the dream-like sensation of being surrounded by people who looked like me — of floating down a mall escalator towards a plaza teeming with hundreds of reflections of myself. But, later, when I try to ask a street vendor for directions, his expression tenses. There is a jolt of confusion before an inevitable realization: he is dealing with an impostor.

*

My mixed feelings towards Asianness are accompanied by an ambivalence in writing about them. Will there be anything here more than meandering narcissism and petty grievance? And if so, what is translating these thoughts into words intended to accomplish?

In *Minor Feelings* — part memoir, part history, part cultural criticism — Cathy Park Hong writes, "I sometimes still feel the subject, Asian America, to be so shamefully tepid that I am eager to change it — which is why I have chosen this episodic form, with its exit routes that permit me to stray. But I always return, from a different angle, which is my own way of inching closer to it."[1]

For me, writing is the best way to engage with Asianness — not just as an identity but also as a gravitational force that I am

---

1. Hong, C. P. (2021). *Minor Feelings: An Asian American Reckoning* (Reprint ed., p. 103). Random House Publishing Group.

pulled by and push against. Like Hong, I am in constant flux.

Moving further from and closer to Asian America, I am balancing my individual desires against my responsibilities to a community. Can I escape rigid cultural expectations without leaving familial ties behind?

Writing is a way of analyzing and reconciling the forces that have shaped my life: language, memory, racial theory, geopolitics, stereotypes, and family. For the most part, the racism I've experienced, both externally and internally, has been mild. Instead of trauma, more of a sense of disorientation, an inability to form an identity beyond what has been defined by my parents and society. To write the personal essay is to create my own frame, to come face to face with the stranger who is myself.

*

My most primal connection to Asianness is rudimentary Mandarin Chinese. Up until middle school, my father taught me the language by recording lessons on a cassette tape. Each night, before bed, I would press play on my sports boombox and listen to his voice reciting a story from a Taiwanese school booklet — realistic tales of children visiting their grandparents or something fantastical like a whole village laboring together to unearth a giant radish. After every sentence, there was a lengthy pause on the tape when I was to repeat the words after him.

Despite my best efforts, I never came close to mastering pronunciation. When I was eight, my parents and I returned to Taiwan. In a marble-tiled living room livened with paintings of flowers and carp, I recited from memory a small Chinese folk tale. Halfway through, looking up from my feet, I saw my aunts and uncles collapsed on the sofa from laughing at my garbled American accent. My cousins, peeking in from the kitchen, gleefully performed imitations of my speech throughout the day.

Conversely, my mother struggled with English. When visiting me at college, she stood impatiently outside of a "coed" bathroom waiting for the password to enter the "coded" room. She had particular trouble with pronouncing R's; my father would ridicule her by performing impressions. At the wheel of the car on a road trip, he passed the time by making up tongue twisters for her to practice. "The duck does not like darrrrrk chocolate," he repeated, to his own amusement, while waiting at a red light.

Even though I stopped speaking Chinese in middle school, it still has a pull on me. Now, it is not so much a language but a series of sounds that evoke a set of memories. When I hear the word for "grape", I remember tottering in the cool shadows of the kitchen, hands full of fruit, and the wonder of biting through translucent

flesh and not finding seeds inside. When I hear the word for "bird",
I am transported to the Taiwanese house of my aunt. The room
is filled with worn sewing mannequins and a red fabric is draped
across a table. A small green and yellow parrot, released from its
cage, hops across the floor like a pebble across water.

What is this strange feeling of relearning a language as you
hear it? Of feeling some deep and vestigial part of your brain kick
and flutter after a few crooked syllables?

In college, my girlfriend, who is White/Jewish, and I would
play a game for my amusement. After eating at an Asian restaurant,
she would open our fortune cookies and read the "Learn Chinese"
section where simple words are listed in their Mandarin characters
and simplified English pronunciations.[2] Like a game of telephone,
she and I would try to form a connection through a language she
didn't speak and one that I had trouble understanding. Scrunching
up her face and laughing helplessly, she attempted various
pronunciations at my encouragement. Usually we gave up after a
few tries but there were occasional successes.

"Egg?" I guessed one night, leaning across the table and
watching the words float off her lips as if that could help.

"You're so close," she said. "What kind?"

---

2. For example: "Kùzi", meaning "pants".

"Chicken egg?" I said.

"Yes! I can't believe it." She clapped her hands together before handing me the fortune. "How did you know?"

"I just felt it in my heart," I said.

*

My favorite memory of Taiwan is a memory of a memory.

When I was young, my mother and I had a hygiene routine. Each month, I would sit in her lap so that she could pick my ear wax with a bobby pin. This is probably an Asian thing but I've been too embarrassed to check with any of my Asian or non-Asian friends. I've never been particularly close with my parents. We rarely hug, express affection, or celebrate birthdays — so this cleaning ritual was a rare moment of intimacy.

That particular summer afternoon, it had been raining nonstop. The sky had turned a noxious yellow color. Seated in my mother's lap, I was soothed by her soapy smell and the feeling of the pin gently rubbing the insides of my ear. I began to drift off, as if descending into a heavy nap. The noise of the rain swelled around me, droplets were hitting the roof and walls so hard that the whole house seemed to thrum. Then from far away her voice and her hand pointing to the water splattering on the deck outside the living room window.

"See the rain?" she said, squeezing my shoulders. "On the fish farm, we used to say the raindrops bouncing off the ground were like shrimp jumping on the deck of a boat."

*

While reading about Asianness, I've come across many personal essays in which Asians denounce racism and express pride in their identity. It has been more difficult to find writing that echoes the ambivalence I feel and frames it in a larger context. The most helpful works have been those that analyze racialization through Sigmund Freud's theory of mourning and melancholy.

According to Freud, mourning is a normal reaction to loss such as that of a loved one or possession. After a finite period of time, the mourner is able to gradually recover and move their energy to other subjects. In contrast, melancholy is a persistent reaction to loss, especially one that resists definition, like that of a country or ideal. Because the conscious mind cannot process what has been lost, the melancholic becomes psychically stuck and often redirects the pain they feel towards themselves.

In *The Melancholy of Race*, Anne Anlin Cheng — professor of English and director of American Studies at Princeton University — describes how melancholy is marked by a "profound ambivalence".[3] Because of unresolved grief, the melancholic is only able to preserve a ghostly or empty version of the lost object that is both adored and loathed. Like my relationship to Asianness, melancholy pits the desires to retain and exclude against each other without reaching a resolution.

In this way, perhaps the masked Asian man in the checkout line, besides being the object of my scorn, was also an alternative version of myself — a lost authentic self that I would never achieve.

*

As a child, I took pride in being Taiwanese. Mainly because it seemed distinct from being Chinese.

When people asked where I was from, I would make them guess and delight at their responses: China, Korea, Japan. "Taiwan," I would reveal, like a punchline. Coming from a country that others knew so little about made me feel mysterious and sophisticated.

My parents began immigrating to America in 1983. They were leaving an island off the coast of China, that was ruled by martial law from 1949 (before my parents were born) to 1987. At the time, this was the longest period of martial law in the world and has since been surpassed by Syria.[4]

---

3. Cheng, A. A. (2001). *The Melancholy of Race: Psychoanalysis, Assimilation, and Hidden Grief* (Race and American Culture) (Revised ed., pp. 8-9). Oxford University Press.

4. A fact I did not know until researching this essay.

After meeting through a village matchmaker, my parents decided my father would immigrate first, studying statistics at North Carolina State University before sending for my mother. I was born during a brief stop in Las Vegas; a week after the C-section, my mother completed the final exam of her Master's program in computer science at the University of Nevada. Soon after, the family moved for the final time to West Windsor, a suburb a few miles south of Princeton, New Jersey.

During my youth, I loved the rare instances when my parents told stories of their early days in North Carolina before I was born: my father and mother hiking in the Great Smoky Mountains or watching vendors sell old carbon rifles at the local farmer's market.

Sometimes my father would linger at the kitchen table after dinner. While finishing his beer, he would reminisce about watching Michael Jordan play college basketball.

"What did he look like?" I asked, eager for descriptions and exciting stories.

"Like this," my father said, and stuck out his tongue.

*

Taiwan, like the early roaming life of my family, is defined by melancholy — simultaneously embraced and rejected by the global community. On the one hand, Taiwan is a model, upstart democracy built peacefully after decades of military dictatorship.[5] Academics even looked to its universal healthcare system for guidance on containing the COVID-19 pandemic.[6,7] Major companies, like Apple and Ford, depend on Taiwanese factories to produce semiconductors for smart phones, sensors, and high performance computing. Despite all this, Taiwan is not recognized as a country by most of its allies, including the United States. Presenting a Taiwanese passport will not gain you entrance into a United Nations Building.[8]

Taiwan's ghostly geopolitical position is due to its contentious relationship with China, which considers the island a renegade province to be reunified with the mainland. Because of this view, any countries seeking diplomatic relationships with China must sever official ties with Taiwan. Thus, Western countries find themselves in the strange position of selling weapons to Taiwan and

5 Bush, R. C. (2021, January 21). *Taiwan's democracy and the China challenge.* Brookings. https://www.brookings.edu/articles/taiwans-democracy-and-the-china-challenge/

6. Summers, D. J., Cheng, D. H. Y., Lin, P. H. H., Barnard, D. L. T., Kvalsvig, D. A., Wilson, P. N., & Baker, P. M. G. (2020). Potential lessons from the Taiwan and New Zealand health responses to the COVID-19 pandemic. *The Lancet Regional Health – Western Pacific, 4,* 100044. https://doi.org/10.1016/j.lanwpc.2020.100044

7. Zhang, C., & Glickman, A. (2020, June 29). *Learning from Taiwan about fighting COVID-19 — and using EHRs.* STAT. https://www.statnews.com/2020/06/30/taiwan-lessons-fighting-covid-19-using-electronic-health-records/

8. Horton, C. (2019, July 22). *Taiwan's Status Is a Geopolitical Absurdity.* The Atlantic. https://www.theatlantic.com/international/archive/2019/07/taiwans-status-geopolitical-absurdity/593371/

relying on its strategic military position to limit China's influence while also denying the island's existence. In this way, I was doubly removed from my heritage — first, being the child of immigrants who rarely talked about their homeland and, second, growing up in a nation that didn't recognize Taiwan as a sovereign country.

*

In middle school, my excitement at being Taiwanese was replaced with ambivalence. Instead of feeling unique, I was lumped into the model minority stereotype. Nearly half my classmates were children of immigrants — mainly from Asian countries like India, Pakistan, China, Japan, and Korea. Our families, emphasizing that academic excellence was the best way of securing an upper middle-class life, pressured us to take as many advanced placement classes as possible and cram for standardized tests.[9] Community gossip — passed along by parents bumping into each other at dinner parties, grocery stores, or the public swimming pool — tracked whose child had earned perfect SAT scores or had been accepted early admission to Harvard.

For me, and other children of immigrants, intense focus on

---

9. This fixation on academics rose to national attention in 2015, when my school district was profiled in The New York Times. The article, titled *New Jersey School District Eases Pressure on Students, Baring an Ethnic Divide,* described students hospitalized due to stress and mental health issues as well as growing tensions between White and Asian parents over how grueling schooling should be.

schoolwork was a way of self-segregating from our White peers. I always seemed to be surrounded by the same group of Asians, many of them my friends, as we shuffled through nearly identical classes, rehearsals, and after school study groups.

Growing up, I occasionally resisted my parents' and community's ideas of a stereotypical Asian — one who was docile, hardworking, and naturally gifted at the sciences. When forced to join the middle school orchestra, I chose to play the double bass, regarded as cumbersome and unappealing, over the violin. "I could barely see or hear you," my mother complained after a concert where I had been seated behind a stage curtain.

In high school, I joined the cross-country team and grew out my hair, which nearly reached shoulder length at times. I dressed shabbily, favoring thinning shirts and bleach-stained pants. To my parents' consternation, I decided to study creative writing at Oberlin College, a small liberal arts institution with a counterculture reputation, instead of enrolling at an Ivy League university.

In the end though, I'm not sure how successful these efforts were at distinguishing me from the studious Asian stereotype. After graduating from Oberlin, I applied to MIT's graduate program in Biology. Post admissions, walking past laboratories filled with other Asians, I felt a mixture of emotions: gratitude and excitement for the chance to perform cutting-edge research, that sensation of eeriness I always experience when surrounded by other Asians, and not quite a sense of resignation but a feeling of yielding to fate.

During my first day in the laboratory, I received an email asking for digital tokens. I had no idea what the request was and thought I might have missed a certification. But on closer inspection, I realized that the message had been sent to me by mistake — it was meant for another Justin Chen, one who worked in the Computer Science department.

*

It is difficult to write about the Asian stereotype without feeling that I should be more grateful. There are many worse fates than having demanding parents who care, perhaps too much, for you or undergoing a strenuous education. My parents, who have had a much harder time in America, rarely complain about the times that they were passed over for a promotion or were the target of racist comments in the street.

But there are still issues with this "privileged" stereotyping. The model minority myth uses the economic and professional success of some Asian American groups to downplay the effect of systemic racism on other minorities. It also covers up a lack of

Asian cultural and political representation — rendering us invisible and minimizing the discrimination that we face.

Because Asians occupy a vague position between "white" and "black", our racialization may be particularly melancholic. We have been lauded as model minorities while our long history of exclusion has been largely forgotten or denied. In particular, the National Origins Act — which barred all immigrants from Asia between 1924 and 1952 — was the first and only federal law to legalize immigration discrimination based on race.

As David L. Eng, Professor of English at the University of Pennsylvania, and Shinhee Han, a psychotherapist at the New School, discuss in *Racial Melancholia, Racial Dissociation*, the history of discrimination against Asian Americans "laid the legal foundation for the emergence of the figure of the 'illegal immigrant' and of 'alien citizenship'".[10]

For Eng and Han, Asian Americans today continue to exist in a suspended assimilation:

"The inability to blend into the American melting pot, suggests that for Asian Americans ideals of whiteness are perpetually strained — continually estranged. They remain at an unattainable distance, at once a compelling fantasy and a lost

---

10. Eng, D. L., & Han, S. (2019). *Racial Melancholia, Racial Dissociation: On the Social and Psychic Lives of Asian Americans* (p. 39). Duke University Press Books.

ideal."[11]

*

In 2016, I watched Chris Rock host a contentious Oscars Awards Ceremony. Leading up to the show, critics had pointed out that, for the second consecutive year, all twenty acting nominees and four of five nominated directors were White. Rock opened his monologue by saying, "I'm here at the Academy Awards, otherwise known as the White People's Choice Awards"[12], before continuing to criticize the lack of diversity in Hollywood. And yet, later in the show, he brought three Asian children onstage, introducing them as accountants who had tabulated the vote results.

Rock's joke calls to mind theories of mimicry and stereotyping discussed by Eng and Han — the idea that, in order to be recognized by mainstream society and even ourselves, Asian Americans must mimic model minority stereotypes.[13] Coming out of college, I had trouble seeing myself as a writer or pursuing a more artistically-inclined career. Instead, I took the more defined

11. Eng, D. L., & Han, S. (2019). *Racial Melancholia, Racial Dissociation: On the Social and Psychic Lives of Asian Americans* (p. 36). Duke University Press Books.

12. Times, T. N. Y. (2016, February 29). Chris Rock's Opening Oscar Monologue: A Transcript. *The New York Times*. https://www.nytimes.com/2016/02/29/movies/chris-rock-monologue.html

13. Eng, D. L., & Han, S. (2019). *Racial Melancholia, Racial Dissociation: On the Social and Psychic Lives of Asian Americans* (p. 45). Duke University Press Books.

path and became a scientist. Not only was I interested in biology but, more importantly, I felt that attending a prestigious graduate school program would earn the approval of my parents and West Windsor's Asian community.

Looking back, I still find Rock's joke more bemusing than insulting. But perhaps I should be more heated. Like discrimination towards Asians, the joke seemed to exist in an ambiguous middle ground between harmless quip and noxious racism. For me, like many Americans, Rock's joke is just inoffensive enough to look past and pretend that it had never happened.

Muting my response to racism has been part of a larger effort to erase my Asianness, to escape the pressure of mimicry or fulfilling expectations. I love my parents but I also tend to keep a distance from them. Since I've left West Windsor, our main connection has been a few short conversations over the phone each month. I've also made it a point to ignore mainstream depictions of Asianness — like the film *Crazy Rich Asians* or the sitcom *Fresh off the Boat* — and avoid serious thought on how being Asian has shaped my life. There is something soothing about being invisible — of being only yourself and by yourself.

I have felt most at peace when running. In high school, I ran 60 miles a week during the summers, mostly at night. I started in the suburbs where illuminated rooms seemed to float in the darkness — the shifting blue light of a television or the prismatic radiance of a chandelier in a foyer — and worked my way out into farmland. I passed acres of rustling corn and the lumpy silhouettes of sleeping cows until I reached almost complete blackness. I never wore any reflective gear, stepping into the grass seconds before a car and its fiery headlights rushed past. I wanted the invisibility, to have the physical sense of being in a void match the experience of being adrift between cultures.

*

The last time I visited Taiwan was in 2013 when I was in my second year of graduate school. This was my fifth trip back but this time was different: my family would be visiting the fish farm where my mother had been raised. It had been more than thirty years since she had left.

My parents' families had gone in opposite directions. When my parents met, my mother's family was uneducated but relatively wealthy due to the success of the fishing industry. My father's side of the family, who lived in the capital city of Taipei, was poorer but held more prestigious jobs as teachers and government workers. In the thirty years since their marriage, my mother's family had fallen on difficult times. During the car ride from the airport out into the countryside, my father recited an inventory of my mother's side: A college graduate, a high school dropout, a middle school dropout.

Stepping out of the car, I was met by an expanse of land. In the city, the sun had been dizzying and kaleidoscopic, reflecting in all directions off of cars, skyscrapers, and store signs. But here it was gently omnipresent, radiating down from the sky to the unbroken view of the horizon. My mother led us through a grid of rectangular ponds dug out of the ground and rimmed with concrete. They were each the size of a soccer field. Row after row after row, they looked like a set of watercolors ranging from green to grey blue to almost white depending on the angle of the sun on the water.

"This is your maternal grandfather's fishpond," my father said, sensing an opportunity for a speech. "They worked all day and night to send your mother to college, which was pretty rare. Then your mother and I worked hard to send you to college. If you fail out of grad school you could come back and work here."

Technically, we were visitors, no one in my family still worked here. They had sold the land to a small group of farmers. One of them, a sixty-year old man with jet black hair, appeared before us on a sputtering motorcycle. Together we walked along the grassy embankments dividing the ponds while he pointed out various details: the motorized paddles near the corners which oxygenated the water, small concrete huts with a single door and window that stored supplies, a patch of bushes where he had hidden to catch poachers stealing crawfish.

My mother didn't talk much during the tour. Most of her comments were observations of the landscape. "Oh, here's the road we used to bike down," she said. "It's still here."

Like someone checking their limbs after an accident, she seemed only to express herself through the presence or absence of things.

My mother and I were only able to discuss the trip and her early experiences in America five years later. And even then, only under the pretense of a formal tape-recorded interview for posterity rather than a more natural heart-to-heart.

"I never wanted to leave [Taiwan] because I couldn't speak English," she said, sitting across from me at the kitchen table. Originally she had thought she might be in the United States for a year until my father completed his Master's degree. But then, he was accepted into a Ph.D. program. "So then Grandma told Dad, 'Continue to study and don't come back.'"

For students, like my father, who had been blacklisted for political reasons, American universities offered the best chance for a successful career. The pressure was intense, as continued enrollment and stipend payments depended on academic performance.

"Everyone studied really hard. They didn't pay attention to their wives," my mother said. "One wife cannot stand this, because she had a good life in Taiwan, so she killed herself in the bathroom. Then all the husbands were nicer to their wives. Every time they came home, they checked the bathroom to make sure it was okay."

"So did Dad check the bathroom for you?" I asked.

"Not really," my mom said, and chuckled.

"But didn't you miss Taiwan?" I said.

"There was no time to miss," my mom said. "I needed to learn a lot of things because everything was new. If you cannot speak English, you have a lot to learn."

After 40 minutes, I asked my mother one final question: Had she ever thought of returning to Taiwan after retiring? I had a fantasy of her reconnecting with family and old compatriots, of not having to struggle to speak the language, of being able to relax into a culture.

"Why would I do that?" she responded. "Everyone I know, all my friends, are here."

*

There will never be a simple way for me, or my parents, to relate to Asianness. Like Cathy Park Hong in *Minor Feelings,* we are constantly straying and returning. Identity is not something we innately possess. It is something that is framed and reframed by the stories we tell ourselves.

After completing my doctorate at MIT in 2018, I left academia to work on the communications team at a healthcare nonprofit. I was redefining myself in many ways. The woman I had been dating for four years ended our relationship and moved out. Most of my friends, fellow graduate students, were leaving Boston in search of academic jobs elsewhere. On the weekends, I would sit in my hollowed-out studio apartment. The morning light, illuminating the white walls and oakwood floors, made my life feel expansive and weightless.

My parents were perplexed by my career change; for several months my father wouldn't acknowledge my new job. But then, a year later, when I was visiting New Jersey during the summer, he seemed to have come to terms with my decision.

"That just the trend," my father said unprompted while driving us to the grocery store. The first generation of immigrants become scientists and mathematicians to earn enough for their children's education. The next generation, who assimilate more into society, become doctors and lawyers. "And then the third generation," my father half-joked, "they are super rich so they become … how do you say this? … bloggers and fashion designers."

"But, whatever you do," my father concluded, "just work hard."

For now, the best I can do is to write. Through writing, I achieve the same meditative void as running. Both actions have a kind of invisibility — of being completely yourself and by yourself. But while running is a form of escape, writing is an act of definition. On the page, the writer has the power to reveal only what they choose to or to become someone else entirely. And even reading your own words is to see yourself anew from a distance.

*

Before we left the fish farm, my family visited my mother's childhood home — a simple, two-story white brick building with a small veranda enclosed by a wall. The house had been abandoned for more than a decade — before entering we had to usher away a stray dog who kept circling back towards the front of the house. Later, we discovered that she had given birth to a litter of puppies in the far corner of the enclosure.

Walking through the first floor, I felt as if we were intruding not on people but time itself. The house was still and bare. All the colors — of the walls, carpeting, wood paneling — were bleached and faded. The heat of the sun through the windows was stultifying as if we were in a greenhouse. My mother ushered us into her old bedroom where the floor was raised into platforms for sleeping. Old tatami mats and bedding had been stowed away in the closets. Wandering back out into an otherwise empty hallway, I noticed a darkly stained, wooden nightstand that seemed out of place. Opening its drawer, I found dozens of pictures of myself as a child. Stacked on top of each other, they were nearly half a foot tall.

"We have to save them," my mother said, as we skimmed through the pile. These were pictures she had mailed to her parents while they were still alive.

In the photos, my younger self was dressed in the bright orange and turquoises of the early 90s. Me, leaning back in a highchair with a fist full of cheerios. A year or two later, in the backyard wearing only underwear with the blank, feral look that young children have. The pile ended with professionally taken elementary school portraits where I, already in glasses by the second grade, posed in front of a velvety blue backdrop.

Seeing the familiar scenes of my childhood framed by the walls of a foreign house was so shocking that I briefly thought the pictures must be of some other child. I felt the dizzying sensation of being both the viewer and the subject. It was like hearing a recording of your voice, where you are at once recognizable and foreign, inside and outside of yourself.

I had never met my mother's parents. They had died when I was still a young child. I tried to imagine what they might have thought of the pictures. Was I instantly familiar or alien to them? Someone to embrace or a phantasm already beyond the reach of family and culture? Although my grandparents had most likely set these photos aside and forgotten them, for a second, I let myself believe, in that moment, that they had deliberately stowed the images away, anticipating the off chance of my return.

READING THE GOOD NEWS
Greg Harris

A t just about the moment Merriam-Webster added "doomscrolling" to its list of new words for 2020 — that moment when many of us were sifting through testimonials from heartbroken Italian doctors, staring at global death rate projections, refreshing the webpages of stores that used to offer masks, and watching garbage-bag-clad nurses wheel bodies into portable morgues — my web searching habits changed. To that point as depressive and panicked as anyone's, they started to take on a new character — just as obsessive but in a new direction: toward the technology of renewable energy.

It started with the search for an affordable electric bike. The impulse was escapist, a waste of money, and I knew it. I had a perfectly good bicycle and perfectly good legs, and live in eastern Massachusetts, a terrain of manageable hills. But staying stuck in place had gotten to me. *Doomscrolling* had gotten to me, and if with an electric motor I could get miles farther out onto the open road with the wind in my helmet, wouldn't that just transform things?

It wouldn't. The eventual ebike I bought followed the path of most of my self-improvement purchases: a brief, thrilling moment in the light, then indefinite storage in the basement. See: breadmaker, unicycle, NordicTrack, etc. You'll have your own list. Let's plan a joint garage sale.

What turned out to be unexpectedly valuable, though, were the web magazines I read while doing research for the ebike. Two elbowed their way into my daily reading habits alongside such stand-bys as *The Atlantic* and *The New York Times*. *Electrek* had one of the most entertaining electric bike reviewers on the internet, Micah Toll, a lanky self-professed "battery nerd" who's clearly having a blast showing up in Finnish design shops or photoshopping himself into electric submarines and other unlikely vehicles from China's Alibaba. The other, *CleanTechnica*, had inconsistent reviews but a deeper technical bench, so you could learn about the physics of energy storage and the advantages of certain gear ratios. In both cases, though, the draw soon became not bicycle research, but a glimpse into possible futures.

Stealing glimpses into possible futures was a great pastime of my youth. My father's career in the U.S. Navy had a shattering effect on friendships and any feeling of community: we moved houses 13 times across 7 different states before I graduated from high school. I was frequently alone and had no idea what to do about it other than get as far away, mentally, as I could. If a book had space exploration and rocket ships and aliens, if it played tricks with gravity and robots, if it speculated on alternate realities and sentinels who guarded civilization from a lonely perch on an outer planet, I was going to read it.

It's hard for me now to sort out why I stopped reading science fiction and fantasy. Adolescence ended and my life grew more my own once I got to college — that was part of it. The four years I spent in one small Ohio town were the longest I'd ever lived in one place; the longest I'd kept friends. Raised literary standards were another part. Salman Rushdie's *Midnight's Children* or Leslie Marmon Silko's *Ceremony* offered a richer magic, and language, than anything I'd found in Asimov or Heinlein.

But the greatest part might have been my internalizing of my studies. The English department at that time was suffused with a critical spirit I'd call Marxo-pessimism, hostile to grand narratives and especially to positivism—by which we meant the naïve, science-y way science-types believed in scientific progress, believed it could be determined with some objectivity that *this,* over here, was better than *that*, over there. Against this we deployed irony, which clapped scare-quotes around concepts like 'freedom' and 'transcendence' and 'progress' and even 'knowledge.' Everything was a text, everything in the eye of the critical beholder, and everything that looked to the positivist like a good thing — the rise of our entire Enlightenment- and industrial- and techno-fueled civilization — was a source of wrong: oppressive, unequal, silencing, monocultural imperialistic rot.

My other major area of focus, Environmental Studies, was, if anything, even more destructive of a sense of possibility. The future consisted of an oncoming climate crisis that would bring steepening waves of natural disaster, pandemics, food and water shortages, refugees, conflicts and ultimately the extinction of civilization along with every beloved animal species. Professors took pains to present this vision of the future as a call to action, not despair — but every case study, as well as my early professional work in the field, in a rainforest reserve in Borneo and a wildlife refuge in Alaska — held copious evidence that human nature was really, really not up to the challenge. In the case of Borneo, it didn't ultimately even feel decent to try. The rainforest inhabitants themselves, the indigenous Dayak we were trying to 'save,' wanted a chance to invest in businesses, to have good schools, and medical facilities, and to be part of global culture. Who were we, a bunch of idealists from richer nations, to tell them no, that's not what you should ask for, these riches we've already got?

It's only a slight oversimplification to say that I've lived the past several decades — cultivated a career, raised a family — with my head down, not expecting much by way of a larger future, of civilizational possibilities.

It's been a good life, but one with a hole where the good news might have been.

*

Trace the word gospel back and you get godspell, the Old English for "good" along with "news," though the sense of "spell" is broader, encompassing any form of storytelling. From the same root we get *spiel* in the sense of a speech prone to repeated delivery, intended to sell somebody on something.

I find myself picturing the ancient Jews who became the first Christians. Witnesses to the death pangs of Israel under the python coils of Roman colonization, they experienced the apparent sundering of God's covenant with their people, their chosenness, their destiny. And then suffered the death of their messiah.

They had to be among the lowest of the low; in a very real sense they were staring down the end of days. Within a short time

Rome would massacre 580,000 Jews to put down the Bar Kochba revolt, march millions more Jews as slaves all the way to Rome, melt down the Great Temple of Jerusalem's golden menorah to pay for finishing the Coliseum, and erase any independent nation of the Jews for the next 2,000 years.

In the midst of this, though, the miracle of Jesus's resurrection, God's promise renewed, a future in a different direction. The message, which would ignite a religion thousands of times bigger than Judaism: humans are full of sin, flawed, but — Good News indeed! — to be redeemed almost despite themselves.

Some people, of course, keep the faith of those early days, and expect to be plucked up and rewarded any moment; most of us keep our heads down, not paying too much attention to the larger future, civilizational possibilities. Ask your average American — inhabitants of the richest, most powerful nation in the history of the planet, self-styled heirs to Rome and Israel both — what they see coming, and surveys show most (and especially most young people) expect things to get worse. Even the optimists will struggle to describe what bright thing we're headed for.

*

Keeping your head down, it turns out, only works until your children start looking up to you and demanding answers. As the climate crisis evolved from experts' predictions into lived reality, as the predicted timeline kept getting shorter for when disastrous sea level rise will drown our Boston-area home, and heat waves and ocean acidification make food production falter, my son Ari tied the pieces together like a dark knot. It enveloped him, and followed him around everywhere, the sense that normal life is busted and staggering amounts of suffering are headed his way. Forget having children of his own; forget having any sense of broad possibilities. Early in his high school career, I found him with his head between his hands, staring at the living room floor. "Does any of this have a purpose?" he asked, meaning the conveyor belt of education — sweeping, now, it seemed, not toward a fulfilling career or family of his own, but toward a dystopian nightmare. "It feels like I was born too late."

It was exactly the truth I didn't want either of us to have to face — the truth I would do anything to keep him from believing. I cast about for months for any form of good news to tell him. While I looked, Greenland's glaciers melted, Arctic ice gave way, coral reefs faced bleach death, and Siberia's permafrost erupted into methane craters.

Then an article in the June 2018 issue of *BioScience* was brought to my attention — and it contained, at last, something like a possibility of future. In "From Bottleneck to Breakthrough: Urbanization and the Future of Biodiversity Conservation," Eric Sanderson, John Walston, and John Robinson sketch a revised metaphor of civilization's apparent dead end. If you're passing through a bottleneck, you will experience — just as you would with the end of days — the walls closing in. The difference is that past the narrow point, there's somewhere to go — a breakthrough into a roomier future. They write:

> Drawing reasonable inferences from current patterns, we can predict that…it is not inconceivable that two centuries from now, the population could be half what it is today and the long-cherished goals of a world where people respect and care for nature may be realized, especially if we act now to foster this eventuality. We argue that these gains might be accomplished not through draconian population policies or ongoing perpetuation of poverty, but rather through the social dynamics of cities.

What do cities do that's so magical? Humanity, concentrated in urban areas, has fewer children, lives in far more energy-efficient ways, generates massively more innovation and therefore wealth, and skews cooperative. With an estimated 70-90% of us in cities, fewer of us overall, and economic growth untethered from material sprawl, our future selves can, without sacrifice, devote more of the earth to wildlife-friendly habitat.

The most hopeful part of their vision is that it doesn't rely on humans spontaneously changing our nature from competitive to cooperative, giving up our ferocious love of status and shopping, returning to stone-age technologies, or suddenly all doing the right thing. We just keep going the way we have been: looking for opportunities and security. Greater urbanization, fewer children, and innovation are already key characteristics of advanced and middle-income economies, and renewable energies are already the cheapest way to get things done. It's going to be a rocky transition, of course, but we can make it better by accelerating key processes like the transition to renewable energy and by playing Noah, trying to bring as many species along as we can, until they (and we) have a chance to recover.

I'm not fully endorsing their math, but I am endorsing the effect of this article on conversations with my son Ari. I don't think he *believes* the bottleneck metaphor — it's a metaphor, after all — but there's just enough future to it that he finds it harder to absolutely despair.

*

Consider the elegance of a leaf. A slender matrix of

chloroplasts and waxy lignin unfurled like a banner in the sun, it guides light toward carefully nested stacks of green pigment, kickstarting a complex transport of electrons in a dance that synthesizes sugars. So plentiful is this process that not only do plants and algae fuel their own vegetative growth, they underwrite nearly every form of symbiote, commensalist, parasite, or predator on earth, right down to everyone you know and love.

Photosynthesis — the gases taken in, the gases given off, the fantastical carbon structures its sugars fuel, from sunflowers to palm trees, seaweeds to redwoods — shaped our atmosphere, and makes complex animals possible.

Now picture humankind's most urgent problem: global warming caused by the buildup of carbon dioxide and other greenhouse gases in the atmosphere. Why did carbon dioxide build up? Because we're drawing from the vast reserves of rotted life under the earth, releasing energy by oxidating those leftover carbon structures — in other words, drilling, and burning, oil and gas.

We have begun trying to get the carbon back out of the air by planting trees, but this is an uncertain process, given that forests are burning with historic fury on our hotter and hotter earth. We have begun trying to move to renewable energy, but the process is slow, and the efficiencies of fossil fuels are hard to beat for many applications. Gasoline has about 100 times the energy density of our current lithium-ion batteries; the average passenger car, fully fueled, contains the energy equivalent of 1000 sticks of dynamite. This means a little gas can get you a long way, whereas it takes a huge battery to get you the same distance.

What if we could engineer our own leaves that draw carbon from the air and use sunlight to synthesize not plant sugars that rot into fuel, but — fuel? Such leaves might draw from the atmosphere the exact same amount of carbon we'd want to burn, turning our fossil fuel use into a closed loop, a sustainable system that need never push the planet out of equilibrium. Further: such leaves could democratize energy production, so that any country could sift the atmosphere as needed for the fuel it needs, easing us away from the political disasters of imperialist petro-states (see, currently: Russia invading Ukraine; Saudi Arabia torturing Yemen; U.S. Congress perverted by oil interests).

This is the kind of possibility that my search for electric bicycles led me to. I'd turn to the pages of *Electrek* or *CleanTechnica* for shopping advice, and end up fascinated by the story of a real-life perpetual motion machine: a mining company's electric dumptruck. They'd figured out that they could load the truck with ore at the top of a mountain, send the heavily weighted thing down to be unloaded at the bottom, and gain enough electricity from its regenerative brakes to power the truck — now empty and lighter — right back up.

The mechanical leaf, too, is real-life. In fact there are competing 'bionic leaf' systems, from a team at the U.S. Department of Energy's Lawrence Berkeley National Laboratory that has figured out how to photosynthesize sunlight and atmospheric carbon into ethanol, to a Harvard-led project that uses sunlight and a leaf-sized silicon wafer coated with metal catalysts to turn water into green hydrogen, pairing the system with genetically engineered bacteria to produce alcohol fuels at a rate more efficient than natural photosynthesis produces sugars. Biochemist Daniel Nocera, the lead researcher on the team, was ecstatic: "I took air plus sunlight plus water and I made stuff out of it, and I did it 10 times better than nature. That makes me feel good."

It felt good to read about it, too. If we are to escape our bottleneck — to achieve what Sanderson writes about as "breakthrough," and not go gently into that good night, oughtn't we do as Dylan Thomas commends, and be "wild men who caught and sang the sun in flight," or even — to make a pastiche of his poetry, harness "the force that through the green fuse drives the flower"?

The search for an electric bike ended, but my reading habits only ramped up. Both *Electrek* and *CleanTechnica* make a grand narrative of Elon Musk's efforts at Tesla to force the electrification of the world's cars (and struggle with his recent megalomaniac whackiness); both follow with glee the milestones by which country after country reaches a tipping point where electric car sales grow, and fossil fuel ones wither; both convey the learning curve on cold-latitude heatpumps and the why-didn't-we-do-this-already innovations like clapping a solar panel canopy over California's water canals, to simultaneously generate electricity and reduce water loss from evaporation in that drought-stricken, absolutely crucial agricultural state.

Their pages — especially *CleanTechnica's* — are full of warnings, of course, about the civilization-threatening mess we're driving ourselves toward, but I find myself seeking these pages as an antidote to the doom elsewhere. Because here's the thing, if you're looking for hope: human nature hasn't changed a whole lot recently, and by recently, I mean over the 4,500 year span for which we have coherent written testimony. Read Machiavelli or Aeschylus, Plato or Confucius, the Mahabharata, the Bible, or the *Tao te Ching*, and you'll find yourself nodding along with the characterizations and the iron laws of human fate. "Fear has two faces: rage and lust," Vyasa proclaims in the *Bhagavad Gita*, and no one since has come up with a truer explanation for figures like Donald J. Trump.

We have, of course, figured out a bunch of things about working together over the centuries — the large-scale democratic cooperation that keeps a United States or an India together has never before been attempted, and if you add together the allied democratic states of Europe and Southeast Asia we have — at least for the time being — good reason to be proud, and statistical evidence to back up the perception that, as much as things feel like they're always ready to fly apart, the amount of conflict, poverty, and early death is dramatically less than it was a century ago. (See: Steven Pinker's *The Better Angels of Our Nature* for the full run-down). But such progress is owed at least as much to technology as it is to politics. It is far easier to stop enslaving other humans when you can run your farm with tractors and combines and wash the laundry and dishes by machine. Far easier to coordinate international diplomacy when you can fly or Zoom in for meetings, rather than send wax-sealed messages by sailboat on uncertain wind.

For transformative progress, then, I've come to look exactly where the Marxo-pessimists of my English Department taught not to: to our science and technology, the arts by which — ever more strongly, ever more rapidly over the past 500 years — we've lifted ourselves, on wings of efficient use of power (soon to be, let's hope, wings of renewable and sustainable power). The very engineering that supports the mass of us and threatens the planet, is the superpower that might save us.

And so I read.

It's clear to me, as I do so, that this Good News is steeply dependent on an element of faith. My reading of *Electrek* and *CleanTechnica* and their cousins might only amount to techno-escapism. However fact-based they may be, articles about perovskites or space-visors made of orbiting bubblewrap might be serving the same role that reading science fiction used to in my adolescence, letting me park my head in a haze of possible futures, instead of trying to cope with present challenges too difficult to confront.

But who's to say which possible future to believe in? It was William James, that ultimate American pragmatist, who argued that when there are living options — credible, compelling possible choices of view — "which the intellect of the individual cannot by itself resolve," we have freedom to believe in those which leave us better off, and no obligation to choose those which would deny us the good of such belief.

I do know I've replaced a portion of my doomscrolling with

the good news on *CleanTechnica* and *Electrek* — that's a meaningful and constructive change in itself. More importantly, I have a spiel prepared now for when my son Ari next asks, is there hope? Let me tell you, I can say. The skies may be dark for now. But picture, out west, a vista across desert mountains. A forest of silvery leaves has unfurled, on trees fashioned with all the craft and ingenuity that human art can muster. These leaves, they tug at the wind, they glitter in the sun. They coax from the air centuries' worth of our mistakes, and they are dewy with a bright and possible future.

Race, Family, and Enduring Histories: An Interview with E. Dolores Johnson about her Memoir *Say I'm Dead*

Artress Bethany White

Pangyrus Nonfiction Editor Artress Bethany White interviewed E. Dolores Johnson, author of *Say I'm Dead, A Family Memoir of Race, Secrets, and Love* (Lawrence Hill Books, 2020) to learn more about her memoir and the tragedy of racism in her family history.

Artress Bethany White: Let me start by saying that I really enjoyed reading *Say I'm Dead.* In your memoir, as you worked through themes of lynching, economic oppression, and racial discrimination — themes that pervade the African American literary tradition. What kept you feeling that your story was worthy of being told amid so many others?

E. Dolores Johnson: The themes of lynching, economics and discrimination are the truth of my family and Black life in America and are vividly portrayed in scene after true scene of *Say I'm Dead, A Family Memoir of Race, Secrets and Love.* The book also deals with the related theme of racism levied against interracial families. In my family, we lived with both kinds of racism, because we have five generations who lived in mixed-race relationships. And that is the uniqueness of this story, that and the portions told from my white mother's point of view differentiate *Say I'm Dead* from so many other books in the canon.

The part of this memoir that people gravitate to is the escape of my white mother and Black father from the 1943 Indiana Klan culture to marry legally elsewhere and hide from Mama's family for 36 years. Yet the beginning of my family's mixed relationships, as in all such relationships in America, began in slavery. In the 1800s, my 15-year-old great grandmother was repeatedly raped by a white man on a plantation. I believe *Say I'm Dead* is a narrative worthy of being told because it stands on the truth of racism yet has a hopeful note when decades later the puzzle pieces of the two sides of my family, and the two sides of myself, come closer together through love. By the two thousand-teens, my Black daughter did what her grandmother never could: marry across the race line without fear. And now my mixed-race grandson is part of census statistics: the growth in mixed-race births outstrips the birth rate for single race babies three-to-one. Yet he must be trained on the racist dangers he will face in America and his role in defeating them. This is, therefore, not the oft-told tragic mulatto story either.

ABW: In your memoir, you poignantly recount being told that college was not for you by your white high school guidance counselor. Thankfully, you were offered and able to accept a full scholarship to Howard University and went on to earn a Harvard MBA. Under your guidance, your daughter attended both Brown University and Princeton. Do you believe that African American students continue to face a level of educational discrimination in this country similar to what you faced in the 1960s?

EDJ: Only through the serendipity of a neighbor telling me to take the scholarship exam for Howard University did I get a college education. Until then, higher education was a closed door to me, a girl whose guidance counselor never looked at her transcript of honors classes, yet said Black girls "don't go to college." Hers was a racism that directed me to take up other women's hems for a living, even though I'd botch every one of them since I got a D in sewing. Winning that four-year, fully paid Howard scholarship changed my life. There, not only was I educated in economics, but the history and issues of Black America. It was the place that gave me the intellectual foundation and personal confidence to go on to Harvard and an executive career. It was the drive for educational success passed on to my daughter. Unfortunately, my experience with that counselor in *Say I'm Dead* has been similarly recounted by many others. In *Becoming*, Michelle Obama's 1980s counselor tells her she is not Princeton material, so shouldn't apply. And yes, this discouragement continues today, according to a 2017 article in *Education Next*, where Johns Hopkins reported that "… white teachers, who comprise the vast majority of American educators have far lower expectations for Black students than they do for similarly situated white students."

ABW: One of my favorite and most compelling sections of your memoir is when you transition from your husband's illness in the aftermath of the cross-burning incident in your front yard in Baton Rouge, Louisiana in the mid-1970s to the childhood event of your parents purchasing their first home in Buffalo, New York. You write deliberately about redlining and the exploitation of Black homeowners. Recently, I found myself considering that home ownership in all-white neighborhoods is proof of the performative nature of liberal white allyship separating political discourse from praxis. I am curious about your thoughts on this assessment considering the experiences of you and your family.

EDJ: My family was devastated by the destruction of the beautiful parkway that attracted us to buy in that certain neighborhood across town from our ghetto. The parkway was replaced within a few years of our arrival by an expressway. It accommodated the white flight people who didn't want to live near us, moved to suburbs, and then had long commutes that inched through rush hour. In *Say I'm Dead*, this disregard of our newly achieved homeownership was but one way that whites maintained de facto segregation across America. The cross burning at my newly purchased Baton Rouge home was another.

Sadly, America's housing remains segregated. Ninety percent of suburban residents are white while many urban areas are majority minority. To my mind, that is a cornerstone of racism's continuing life. Segregated housing means segregated schools, which means different races have little opportunity to know each other and form relationships that can overthrow underlying stereotypes, fear and doubt.

Once established in my career, I chose to live in white suburbs for two reasons: better schools for my child and rising property values. One of my white neighbors expressed surprise at my economic and educational standing among them, which signaled a lack of understanding of Black success. We all got along. But when

HUD proposed affordable housing in that town, people fought it, not understanding the motive to make teachers and first responders able to afford to live there. As to allyship, the question is not whether some whites have the intention of learning about racism, but what are they willing to give up to eradicate some of it.

ABW: In the latter third of your memoir, you compare the lives of your white ancestors to that of your African American forebears. You note that, "My maternal grandmother was raised by a striving craftsman who chose to immigrate to America for a better life, plying his trade freely in the late 1800s while my Black sharecropper great grandmother was being raped by a plantation white man." You use these situational and economic realities to graphically depict the historical economic inequity between white and Black Americans. How do you see an acknowledgement of this history ending "opportunity privilege" in this country?

EDJ: Thanks for calling out that passage. I wanted readers to understand the root of today's inequities, back to that real 1800s difference in my own family. Those who have read that section of *Say I'm Dead* have yet to comment on it. Feedback thus far has been an overall condemnation of the racism my family experienced, but I'm afraid acknowledgement of racial inequities will not end "opportunity privilege!" At this current moment of racial reckoning, America is only beginning to know the history and impact of inequities. Knowing precedes acknowledging, which precedes actions that can change the status quo.

ABW: As I read your book, I thought about my own literary journey to discover more about my family's American enslavement and white genealogical ancestry. When I tested my DNA, I ended up being of 28% European ancestry, yet for me to claim myself as a white citizen would be ludicrous on multiple levels, starting with the fact that I am a brown-skinned woman. When you carried out your own DNA test, you tested 75% European ancestry. Do you attribute your grounding in your African American selfhood as a combination of a more realistic acceptance in the Black community of a history of enslavement leading to a logically diverse color palette as well as a devotion to your more brown-skinned father and his race experiences in America?

EDJ: Throughout American history, people mixed with Black and white have been considered Black. That started with slavery too, when Massa fathered mixed offspring; he counted them as additions to his slave holdings, not family. Hence the Black community is still where mixed people are included and comfortable, rather than white ones. Though DNA says I am 75% white, I, like in Caroline Randall Williams's *New York Times* article,

"…am a confederate monument." What tips my DNA into mostly white is my great grandfather, the plantation rapist, whose blood repulses me. What has formed my dominant identity is both the racism my family and I endured and my four years at Howard University where Black pride, achievement and activism took root in my purpose.

ABW: Once you understood that your parents' marriage was a secret one, your memoir becomes largely about finding your white relatives as a means of coming to a better understanding of your biracial identity. Was it your desire that readers walk away from reading about your journey with a surety that embracing difference carries fewer pitfalls than holding onto traditionalist racial baggage?

EDJ: After learning so much by tracing my father's genealogy, I felt the hole in me from not knowing anything about my mother's half of my heritage. The idea of biracialism wasn't on the table in 1979 when I searched for them because there was no permission to be half white in America. There was no telling what reaction her family would have when I showed up. The beauty of my story is that the fear, secrets and separation my parents lived with because of systemic racism did not hold up on the personal level when we found Mama's white family. So, I embraced my white family, my half who decided love trumps race. *Say I'm Dead* shows America can bring the races together, though I cannot assure you of how that will happen or what the price of getting there will be.

———————

E. Dolores Johnson is the author of *Say I'm Dead, A Family Memoir of Race, Secrets, and Love* (Lawrence Hill Books, 2020), a multigenerational memoir that shows America's changing attitudes toward mixed race families through the courageous journeys of the women in her family. Dolores was born in Buffalo, NY. She earned degrees from Howard University and Harvard Graduate School of Business in Boston. Johnson is a published essayist focused on inter-racialism. She lives in Cambridge, Massachusetts. To learn more about her and her work, visit her website www.edoloresjohnson.com or follow her on Twitter @e_dolores_J, Instagram @edoloresjohnson and FB Dolores Johnson.

MAY YOU RISE TO IT:
A LOVE LETTER TO STUDENTS IN AN UNPRECEDENTED TIME

Timothy Patrick McCarthy

End of March, 2020

My dear students,

Let me say this first: I love you — and I hope all of you are somewhere safe right now.

I know this doesn't find any of us well. This global pandemic has profoundly upended our lives and livelihoods and routines and responsibilities, to say nothing of our capacity to work and dream together to build a better world. The corona crisis has catapulted us into complete chaos, accompanied by a disorienting mix of emotions: fear and despair, anxiety and anger, uncertainty and longing, concern and compassion. If you are like me, you're experiencing all these things at once on any given day. As one friend put it: "I didn't realize I could have so many mood swings before my first cup of coffee." As a historian, I rarely use the word *unprecedented* — after all, almost everything has some kind of precedent — but I dusted it off last week and have been using it more and more with each passing day. History will have time to take full account of this moment, but first we must survive it.

And I want to believe we will.

Over the last two weeks, I've been in touch with many of you, and I know you're not okay: I know you're freaking out; I know you're feeling sick; I know you're sad and disappointed and angry and anxious; I know you can't afford to go home; I know you don't feel safe at home; I know you don't have a home or know where home is right now; I know your work life is precarious; I know you worry about being able to pay bills; I know you're worried about money and financial aid and student loans and debt; I know you don't know if you can go to school next year; I know you're worried about visas; I know they're closing borders and banning travel; I know you're worried you won't be able to come back; I know you want to stay here; I know you don't want to stay here; I know you don't have documentation; I know you're worried about being targeted; I know you have pre-existing conditions; I know you're more susceptible to this virus; I know you don't have reliable health care; I know you're on the front lines of this; I know you're worried about your families, both given and chosen; I know you have to work and homeschool your kids; I know you can't afford child care; I know you have to take care of your parents; I know your summer plans are cancelled; I know your first years and final years of school have been ruined; I know you don't know what your acceptances mean right now; I know you don't want to take classes online; I know you don't have reliable internet access; I know you don't want to continue taking classes at all; I know you worry about grades; I know you want to know why anyone is still giving grades; I know you're mourning the loss of sports seasons and artistic productions, proms and parties, graduations and commencements; I know you don't know what to do; I know none of this makes any sense; I know you feel like too many of our leaders are failing; I know you wish you had some warning; I know you still want to mobilize and organize and protest; I know you want to work on a campaign; I know you are worried about the election; I know you want to burn it down; I know you want to build something up; I know you want to be useful; I know you want to know when it will all be over; I know how many of you feel alone right now; and I know you are searching for some kind of hope. I am, too.

For what it's worth, and I also know this isn't nearly enough right now: I hear you.

To be honest, I know many more things about you than I ever knew a few weeks ago. I'm overwhelmed by it, too, but let me just say this: I'm here for you, whatever that means moving forward, because once you're my student, you're always my student. We're all making this up as we go along right now — no one should pretend otherwise — including your teachers and administrators, who are trying their best, along with everyone else, to figure this madness out in real time, moment by moment. For the time being, let's try to trust each other more than we have before, rely on each other as best we can, and ask each other for help however and whenever we need it. This is not the best time to work out pre-existing acrimonies and resentments and suspicions, as longstanding or legitimate as they may be. We have an opportunity, *right now*, to try to be the best version of ourselves. Never has a tired cliché been closer to the truth: *we're in this together.*

Most of you probably don't know how much I love to write letters. Back in the day, I wrote letters all the time. In middle school and high school, I often got in trouble for passing letters — and also talking too much — in class. (This is the *real* "origin story" of my communications "expertise"!) Both my grandmothers were legendary letter writers. My paternal grandmother — the Irish side — was a trailblazing educator, the oldest of sixteen immigrant children and first in our family to go to college, who wrote epic letters to her many siblings, students, and friends. She kept all their responses in shoeboxes in her dusty attic — an archive, of sorts, of their lives. (This was, in fact, the very first archive I ever discovered, after she passed away from cancer the spring of my freshman year of high school.) My maternal grandmother — the Italian side — was a tireless factory worker, a "cuffer" on the garment assembly line who earned her GED when I was a teenager, who wrote to me regularly when I was in college and graduate school. She always apologized for her handwriting and misspellings, but now I'm ashamed to say that I always spent the few dollars she tucked into each of those envelopes without keeping her letters or writing her back. (That archive, alas, is lost.) My resolution this new year was to write several letters each day, in part, as an overdue tribute to my late, beloved grandmothers, but also as a rebellion against our unrelentingly digital world. I promised myself I would hand-write regular affirmations — sincere expressions of gratitude — to the many people in my life who have made and sustained me over the years. I bought nice cards and cute stationary and fun stamps, and I wrote dozens of letters to friends and family in January and February, before life got too busy again. One rarely has the chance — or inclination — to renew one's abandoned resolve, but as my mother likes to say: "The Lord works in mysterious ways." Here we are.

*

My favorite type of letter is a love letter, the most recent of which is here, to my 10-year old niece Malia. She has not yet read it, but she will someday, when the time is right. My forthcoming book, *Stonewall's Children*, is also a love letter of sorts — to the past, present, and future of queer folks. Only a few people have read the entire manuscript so far, but everyone will have the chance to do so when it's published next year. By definition, love letters are usually private affairs, and most of them don't see the light of day, if they ever do, until long after they're written. (I wonder how many love letters have died in dusty attics — or draft folders?) I suspect people are afraid to write them because they're afraid to be vulnerable, exposed or "outed" in some way, which is perfectly understandable, yet profoundly tragic. Fear always is. But then, without warning, an unprecedented fear hits us all in *real* time, and we realize we cannot wait for the *ideal* time. To be honest, I wish everyone would write a love letter to someone right now. More than ever, I believe love letters — both private *and* public — can sustain us, even save us, at a time when fear threatens to undo us.

If you couldn't already tell, this is my love letter to all of you.

Because I'm your teacher, I want to respond to — repay, reciprocate — the things you have shared with me and taught me in the past few weeks. In her recent book, *Can We Solve the Migration Crisis?*, my dear friend and colleague Jacqueline Bhabha, citing the two characters that constitute a single word, reminds us that "crisis," in Chinese, is both *danger* and *opportunity*. We are rightly preoccupied right now with the dangers associated with this crisis, which are serious and many. But let me focus instead on the opportunities it affords us to *build community, find compassion,* and *stay critical.* In the absence of a vaccine or cure, which we know will be slow in coming, these are the best antidotes we have to get us through this current crisis.

As you know, I have always believed that the classroom can and should be a *community.* Throughout my teaching career over the last 25 years, I have tried to cultivate and curate this as best I can, and we've built community together over and over again. We have done so by getting to know each other, giving each other equal air time, listening as much as we talk, devoting ourselves to the work, and respecting each other's different perspectives and opinions, even and especially when we don't understand or agree with them. We haven't always done this perfectly — I'll be the first to admit my own mistakes and missteps along the way — but we've worked hard at this for a very long time now. This has been one of the great blessings of my life, and it has taught me many invaluable lessons that I am leaning hard on to get me through this. Classroom community is obviously easier to foster when we're face-to-face, in the same space over a sustained period of time. This is the magic that makes education worth its frustrations and imperfections, even in the best of circumstances. In this time, which is hardly that, when we are confined to virtual spaces for the foreseeable future, building community is a powerful and profound challenge. For what it's worth, my colleagues, myself included, are doing our best to adapt to these difficult times and damn technologies, as are you, with little warning on an unforgiving timeline. For what it's worth, never in my life have I seen more educators — at every level, in every place I teach and well beyond them — reaching out to one another for ideas and support. As students, you should know this. Please have patience with your teachers, and find ways to connect with us to keep this education going. Frankly, I see this as an unprecedented opportunity, a silver lining of sorts, for all of us to enlist each other in re-imagining teaching and learning on every level. As tempting as it may be for both students and teachers to give up on classes right now — to call it a semester and hope for a "do over" or "reset" next year — I think this is actually an *ideal* time, in less than ideal circumstances, to transform our classrooms into the communities we want and need and deserve. Perhaps this is even a moment to flatten a different kind of curve: the ancient hierarchies and arbitrary evaluations, the unnecessary competitions and unhelpful conflicts, that so often get in the way of building the best and bravest classroom communities. In this time of "social distancing," which also threatens to be a time of isolation and alienation for so many people, let's log on rather than check out. As I have witnessed time and again these past few weeks — through FaceTime check-ins with family, Zoom happy hours with friends, Google organizing calls with fellow activists, GoTo webinars and Facebook Live events with strangers and kindred souls, and all sorts of sessions on all these platforms with many of you — these virtual spaces can produce real communities if we're willing to stay connected to each other and do this hard work together.

The strongest communities are rooted in *compassion*. Even before this virus hit, a common claim had caught hold: "this country has never been more polarized." As a historian of politics and social movements in the United States, I have been quick to counter this claim, asking people if they've ever read the fierce Constitutional debates of the late 18th century that gave birth to the nation, or if they've ever studied the ferocious debates over slavery in the 19th century that brought the nation to its brink, or if they've ever heard of, say, the 1930s or 1960s or 1980s or 2000s. While historically accurate — we've *definitely* been polarized before, and there's ample precedent to prove this — my "push back" is also, on some level, I suppose, an act of intellectual and political arrogance. (It depends on the tone and the day.) But for what it's worth, though sometimes snarky, it is intended to trump (as it were) those who live foolishly in the present without regard for the past, or those who long feverishly for a past that never really existed. After all, navel gazing and nostalgia, when left to their own devices, are *always* dangerous. That said, there is no denying that we're living in an age where the pendulum of public discourse has been swinging aggressively back and forth between various poles of identity and ideology and inequality. I have certainly taken my turn, whenever I had the opportunity, to push the pendulum hard in the direction I prefer. I don't apologize for this, since I've spent too much of my life playing Sisyphus. (You'll have to excuse me for mixing metaphors, it's a weird time.) One response to these severe pendulum swings, so common in our schools these days, is the call for "civility," as if this should be the mandatory "middle ground," a requirement for our continued inclusion and belonging, rather than a serious moral aspiration that needs to be hard earned, especially by those who have not yet done their share of the pushing when it comes to things like equality, freedom, rights, and justice. (Or bending, if you prefer to quote Dr. King, as so many seem to do, on the "arc of the moral universe.") That said, this unprecedented moment in history demands not superficial calls for "civility," which can sometimes feel like a weapon used to silence, but a more serious commitment to compassion. And by this, I mean more consistent attempts at deep understanding and acts of loving empathy that can lead us in the direction of sustained solidarity with people who are suffering — in this immediate instance, those who have been diagnosed with COVID-19; those who have already died or lost loved ones; first responders and other *essential* workers who are on the frontlines of this crisis; anyone whose basic needs of food, water, work, wages, housing, and health care are not being met; those who are always more susceptible to disease and death during times like these precisely because they've never had their fair share of these things; and folks who have not yet endured this crisis but surely will. I have been thinking a lot recently about the AIDS crisis, which decimated the LGBTQ community during the 1980s and 1990s, when I was growing up, and has plagued the globe ever since. One of the reasons HIV/AIDS became a pandemic in the first place is because those who were most deeply affected — infected, "positive" — were stigmatized as social pariahs, *disposable people.* This is still the case with too many people in too many places. For the greater part of a decade during the so-called "Reagan era," there was a deadly lack of compassion (and political action) for "those people," many of whom, it turns out, were *my* people. Though dangerous, and devastating in its death toll, the AIDS crisis in its early stages also produced an opportunity for queer people to act up and demand everything from basic human recognition and rights to antiretroviral drugs and real political power. As Prior Walter declares at the end of Tony Kushner's *Angels in America*, a play that quite literally saved my life in those days: "This disease will be the end of many of us, but not nearly all, and the dead will be commemorated and will struggle on with the living, and we are not going away." During that time, as I have learned from my elders, our community was certainly not without conflict, even "incivility." Nevertheless, we found a way to be compassionate with ourselves and care for one another at a time when no one else would. This is one reason why many of us, though not nearly all, were eventually able to survive that plague. It's also why the LGBTQ community has something to teach the nation and the world right now about how to find compassion in the midst of crisis. When it comes to matters of life and death, we can ill afford to close the borders of understanding, empathy, and solidarity at the boundaries of identity, ideology, and inequality. If ever there were a time to be compassionate bridge builders and boundary crossers, this is it.

As radically committed as we should be in this moment to building community and finding compassion, we must also stay *critical*. The corona crisis has inspired many exhortations to "not make this political." On some level, I suppose, I understand the intention behind this. The last thing we should do right now is search for any and every excuse to fight for its sake, and we should certainly resist any peer pressure to root for folks to fail. That said, the call to avoid politics in this moment is not only the wrong message, it's a dangerous one. This is especially true for those of us who care about history and government, leadership and communications, social movements and human rights, race and class, gender and sexuality, public service and global development, or any of the other things we have studied together over the last generation. Moments of crisis, whether "natural" or human-made, always place into sharp relief the pre-existing conditions of inequality and injustice in any given society. Whenever people experience widespread anxiety and suffering due to something like a pandemic, access to basic human needs — food and water, housing and medicine, work and pay — depends on where we are already positioned in the always vicious and often violent hierarchies that structure our world. And whenever basic human needs are not being provided or protected, human rights are being violated. Many recent commentators have been quick to point out that coronavirus is a "great equalizer," citing well-known celebrities and other well-positioned "elites" who have tested positive alongside "ordinary people." But the deeper truth is that this pandemic is a great *un*-equalizer. Its most devastating ravages — at once physical, material, and emotional — will disproportionately impact those who are most vulnerable: those who are immunocompromised or incarcerated; those who are living in poverty or lacking in health care; those who are stateless or undocumented or housing insecure; those who routinely experience discrimination or isolation; those who are unemployed or working paycheck to paycheck. In the current case of the coronavirus, these things are abundantly clear. What's also clear is that our most powerful institutions — governments and civil society organizations, hospitals and schools, militaries and marketplaces — are inadequately prepared and ill-equipped to deal with this most recent global health crisis. This is no time to retreat from politics or trade in false equivalencies when it comes to our elected officials or political parties. Indeed, it is also no time to think that just because we are all in this together that we are in this together *in the same way*. Just as pre-existing health conditions make some people more susceptible to illness, pre-existing social conditions (including health) make some people more vulnerable to everything — *especially* in times of crisis. And *all* of this is political. We are living through a global case study, in real time, where protagonists and antagonists, failures and successes, injustices and inequalities, power and privilege, best practices and worst practices are already revealing themselves. Make no mistake, this is a generation-defining moment in world history, unprecedented in real ways, and your generation will inherit whatever is to come. You will have to confront the big questions about the size and scope of governments, the rights and responsibilities of citizens, the distribution of resources and capacity of markets, the morality of systems that sort and separate us, the sustainability of our way of life, the undeniable interconnectedness of us all, and so many other things that impact people and the planet we struggle to share. The sooner you gain clarity and muster bravery in the face of all this the better. I want to believe we'll survive this moment because we still have so much more work to do. For what it's worth, I promise to be with you in that work for as long as I am still here.

I have started and stalled and circled back to this letter for more than a week now. To be perfectly honest, I have never felt less useful in all my life than I do in this moment. But I am a teacher, so let me close with all I got: I love you and want you to be okay.

During times of crisis, I always find my way home again to James Baldwin's *The Fire Next Time*. I first encountered this book a generation ago, shortly after Baldwin himself went to his final home. I was around the age some of you are now. Over those many years, for a variety of reasons, it has become something of a sacred text for me. I am certainly not alone in this. After re-reading it last week for what seems like the hundredth time, I want to share the passage that my husband CJ and I chose as a reading for our wedding almost nine years ago:

"It is the responsibility of free men to trust and to celebrate what is constant — birth, struggle, and death are constant, and so is love, though we may not always think so — and to apprehend the nature of change, to be able and willing to change. I speak of change not on the surface, but in the depths — change in the sense of renewal. But renewal becomes impossible if one supposes things to be constant that are not — safety, for example, or money, or power. One clings then to chimeras, by which one can only be betrayed, and the entire hope — the entire possibility — of freedom disappears."

Four constants: birth, death, struggle, love. Birth we have, death will come, and the struggle, of course, continues. Love is ours to choose. And choose it we must — because you, dear students, are my hope for the deep change we need in this unprecedented time.

May you rise to it.

Love always, Tim

PLAY LIKE A GIRL
A REVIEW OF *HAIL MARY: THE RISE AND FALL OF THE NATIONAL WOMEN'S FOOTBALL LEAGUE*
Aime Card

Eleven seniors and eleven juniors faced off against each other on a crisp fall day in a Nashville suburb. The high school had a football infatuation reminiscent of *Friday Night Lights*, crowds of thousands would show up for the games including cheerleaders with major dance routines and a professional announcer simulcasting on local airways. But this game wasn't like that. It was the annual powder puff game for the girls. It took place during a break in the middle of the school day and was held on a sloping side field between the classrooms and the baseball diamond.

The school didn't take the game seriously, but we did. We seniors were out to dominate. We had enlisted a few friends from the boys' football team to coach us and donned their jerseys and eye black to complete the effect. I was a linebacker, and I dug my fingers into the grass as we bent down for the snap. Adrenaline pumped through my veins, and I thought this must be what the boys felt every Friday. I understood the attraction.

Our coaches yelled instructions from the sidelines and our friends cheered as the game got heated. I don't remember if we won or lost, but that wasn't the point. In the end, we slung our arms around each other as we walked off the field, grass stained and sweaty, wiping away tears because it was over: Our only chance to play like the boys.

That day in Nashville was over thirty years ago but came back in a flash the moment I picked up *Hail Mary: The Rise and Fall of the National Women's Football League* by Frankie de la Cretaz and Lyndsey D'Arcangelo (Bold Type Books, 2021). *Hail Mary* is a detailed account of the short period of time during the 1970s that our country had a professional women's football league. Through thorough research and extensive interviews with the players, D'Arcangelo and de la Cretaz paint a vivid picture of this extraordinary venture with historical context and play-by-play action.

Hail Mary highlights issues that have echoed throughout the history of women's sports, primarily the struggle to be taken seriously. The narrative takes the readers through the complete span of women's football, diving into characters like Sid Freeman, "the P.T. Barnum of Women's Football" who organized a collection of teams at first as a gimmick, then as a money-making endeavor. Then follows the origins of the National Women's Football League's major teams, the Toledo Troopers — the winningest team in all of football history, male or female — the Dallas Bluebonnets that played in the home of the Dallas Cowboys, and the L.A. Dandelions that garnered the lion's share of national media attention due to their location. Close profiles of Troopers star Linda Jefferson who rushed for nearly nine thousand yards in her career, and Dandelion's quarterback Rose Low, a first generation Chinese-American who hid her participation from her parents until a promotional appearance on The Merv Griffin Show won their approval, along with dozens of other compelling stories bring to life the complete narrative of the league.

I met with *Hail Mary* co-author Lyndsey D'Arcangelo, and we discussed the frustrating disparity between the coverage and funding of men's and women's sports. "There's still a lot of hurdles for us to get over as far as equity in women's sports, to this day," Lyndsey said.

Due to the lack of documentation and prior research, most of the authors' research was done sifting through old newspaper articles, and Lyndsey shared her exasperation at what they both found. "Frankie and I would copy and paste articles to each other of what people wrote, mostly men, and it was downright appalling. It got old real fast."

Many of the articles tried to pin some kind of motive on the athletes, claiming that they were trying to be like men, or they wanted to prove a point, but the players unilaterally disagreed. "They just wanted to play," Lyndsey said, "it was as simple as that."

In the book the authors write that while most of the players didn't identify with the feminist movement (or Women's Liberation Movement, as it was frequently called at the time), they were a part of it, "simply by living their truths. In that way, they are like countless other women throughout history who never set out to change the world but did so anyway, just because they had the courage not to take no for an answer or accept the role that society told them they should hold."

"They didn't complain about getting paid pennies, or not getting paid at all, lack of proper equipment, and poor travel accommodations because they took what they could get at the time. But times have changed," write the authors. This is clearly evident in the 2022 hard fought and settled lawsuit by the U.S. Women's Soccer Team resulting in a multi-million dollar payout and a promise of equal pay going forward.

The power of bringing stories like this to light is to build on our forward progress. "These women deserve to be recognized," Lyndsey said. "It's also a part of history, not just sports history, but history in general. It's a story that I think can resonate with young women athletes today in a big way."

I agree. In my town's youth flag football league, there have been several all-girls teams, and plenty of girls that played on the boys' teams too. These children could be a part of the progress that carries through high school and collegiate athletics straight into professional sports. The women of the NWFL pushed through all of the ridicule, derision and exploitation and paved the way for the girls and women on the fields today. There are plenty of barriers left to break, but if we link arms with sister athletes past and present, young and old, we can give each other the power to push ahead yard by yard.

CONTRIBUTORS

Jabari Asim is the author of eight books for adults — including *We Can't Breathe: On Black Lives, White Lies,* and *the Art of Survival* — and thirteen books for children. His most recent novel, *Yonder,* was published in 2022. He is the Emerson College Distinguished Professor of Multidisciplinary Letters and director of the MFA program in creative writing.

Aime Card is the author of *And Beneath It All Was Love* (2016), a memoir about her experience with breast cancer, and *The Tigerbelles: One American Team that Set the Pace for Women's Sports* (Lyons Press 2023) about a women's track team in 1960 and their journey to the Olympics from her hometown in Nashville. Aime serves as a Board Member for the Women's National Book Association, Boston Chapter, as well as other community and educational organizations. More at aimecard.com and on Twitter @ aimealleycard.

Justin Chen lives in Philadelphia, Pennsylvania, and works in nonprofit communications. His writing has appeared in *The New York Times* "Modern Love" Column, *Creative Nonfiction's True Story* series, *Essay Daily, Entropy,* and elsewhere. He was the 2020 writer-in-residence at Porter Square Books, his local independent bookstore.

Robbie Gamble's essays have appeared in *Solstice, Soundings East, Tahoma Literary Review,* and *Under the Gum Tree.* He was the winner of the 2017 Carve Poetry prize, and was a Fellow at the Kenyon Writers Workshop. He worked many years as a nurse practitioner caring for homeless people in Boston.

Greg Harris was born in Boston and received his MFA in Creative Writing from Oregon State University. He has taught writing at Harvard University since 2003. Greg has been the recipient of a Fulbright Fellowship and grants from the National Endowment for the Humanities and Oregon's Regional Arts and Culture Council. His audio recording "Champion of Hot Peppers" won a 2001 National Parenting Publications Association Gold Medal for storytelling. His translation of Seno Gumira Ajidarma's novel *Jazz, Perfume, and the Incident* was published as part of the Modern

Library of Indonesia (2012). He has published essays in *The Washington Post, The Boston Globe*, and elsewhere.

E. Dolores Johnson is the author of *Say I'm Dead, A Family Memoir of Race, Secrets, and Love* (Lawrence Hill Books, 2020), a multigenerational memoir that shows America's changing attitudes toward mixed race through the courageous journeys of the women in her family. Dolores was born in Buffalo, NY. She earned degrees from Howard University and Harvard Graduate School of Business in Boston. Dolores is a published essayist focused on inter-racialism. She lives in Cambridge, Massachusetts. To learn more about her and her work, visit her website www.edoloresjohnson. com or follow her on Twitter @e_dolores_J, Instagram @ edoloresjohnson and FB Dolores Johnson.

Ananda Lowe is a Black and multiracial writer and single parent living in Somerville, MA. She is the author of *The Doula Guide to Birth: Secrets Every Pregnant Woman Should Know* (Penguin Random House) and several essays for *NPR*. Ananda is a 2017 graduate of the Memoir Incubator at GrubStreet writing school, and is the recipient of two writers' grants.

Timothy Patrick McCarthy is an award-winning scholar, educator, and activist. He holds a joint faculty appointment in Harvard's undergraduate honors program in History and Literature, the Graduate School of Education, and the John F. Kennedy School of Government, where he is Core Faculty and Director of Culture Change & Social Justice Initiatives at the Carr Center for Human Rights Policy. Educated at Harvard and Columbia, Tim is the author or editor of five books from the New Press, including *Stonewall's Children: Living Queer History in the Age of Liberation, Loss, and Love,* forthcoming next spring. His essay "Coming of AIDS" was published in *Pangyrus* in January 2015. "Provincetown Sketches" is the first installment in a series of creative nonfiction pieces about contemporary queer life in Provincetown, Massachusetts.

Grace Segran was a global nomad and business journalist before settling down in Boston, MA to hone her craft in creative writing. Her personal essays have appeared in the *L.A. Times, Pangyrus, The Common, Brevity Blog, The Smart Set, Cognoscenti,* and elsewhere. She is the winner of the 2019 and 2020 Keats Literary Contests and the winner of Pangyrus's 2021 Nonfiction Contest.

Amy Shea is an essayist with a PhD in Creative Writing from the University of Glasgow, where she has written a creative nonfiction book titled *Not All Deaths are Created Equal.* Her work has appeared in *The Massachusetts Review, The Portland Review, Spry Literary Journal, Fat City Review, From Glasgow to Saturn,* & *the Journal of Sociology of Health & Illness.* She works as the Writing Program Coordinator for Mount Tamalpais College, a junior college for the incarcerated people of San Quentin.

Anri Wheeler is a writer, social justice educator, and mother to three strong daughters. She is a graduate of GrubStreet's Memoir Incubator and VONA, and is working on a memoir about race, class, and mermaids. Her essays and reviews have appeared in *Lit Hub, The Boston Globe, Cognoscenti, Hippocampus, The Brevity Blog,* and others. More at anriwheeler.com.

Artress Bethany White is a poet, essayist, and literary critic. She is the author of the poetry collection *My Afmerica* (Trio House Press, 2019), and the debut essay collection *Survivor's Guilt: Essays on Race and American Identity,* which received a 2022 Next Generation Finalist Indie Book Award. Her prose and poetry have appeared in such journals as *Harvard Review POERTY, Tupelo Quarterly,*

The Hopkins Review, Pleiades, Solstice, Poet Lore and others. White has received the Mary Hambidge Distinguished Fellowship from the Hambidge Center for Creative Arts for her nonfiction, The Mona Van Duyn Scholarship in Poetry from the Sewanee Writers' Conference, and writing residencies at The Writer's Hotel and the Tupelo Press/MASS MoCA studios. She is associate professor of English at East Stroudsburg University in Pennsylvania.